PRINCIPLES OF
Commercial Real Estate
MORTGAGE SERVICING

Mortgage Bankers Association of America

Dearborn
Real Estate Education

This publication is designed to provide accurate and authoritative information in regard to the subject matter covered. It is sold with the understanding that the publisher is not engaged in rendering legal, accounting, or other professional services. If legal advice or other expert assistance is required, the services of a competent professional person should be sought.

Senior Vice President & General Manager: Roy Lipner
Publisher: Evan Butterfield
Development Editor: Anne Huston
Production Manager: Bryan Samolinski
Senior Typesetter: Janet Schroeder
Creative Director: Lucy Jenkins

chapter 4   **Escrow Analysis 27**

chapter 5   **Financial Statements 49**

chapter 6   **Property Inspections 63**

chapter 11   Commercial Mortgage-Backed Securities 113

While our society is a service society, the meaning of the term "service" seems to be understood by all but practiced by few. To be sure, certain industries display the requirements of "good service" more than others. One billion-dollar sector of our economy delivers quality service every business day. That sector is, of course, the commercial banking industry. That industry delivers service from the initiation of a developer's concept to the closing and all-important servicing of the commercial real estate loan. All the requirements of the principal players must be met in a professional and timely fashion or the transaction will fail.

Commercial real estate assets are continually bought, sold, developed, and redeveloped. This makes real estate investment one of the nation's most active and important business activities. There are several types of investors, all with different criteria, all with different values, all with an assortment of analytical tools. However, all have the same objective in mind: the successful acquisition, financing, holding, and/or disposition of commercial real estate within their own definition of the profit motive.

The commercial mortgage banker must be prepared to meet the significant challenges of the current market. The demands of knowledge and service are stringent, be they in loan origination, institutional coordination, documentation, underwriting, servicing, securitization, analysis, or governmental interaction. These demands may originate from the investor or from institutional lenders themselves. All have a role and all require dependable response.

Change is constant, and it is very evident in the specialized and now highly technical specialty of servicing commercial real estate loans. Loan administration serves as the "back office operation" of the mortgage banker. The service provider protects the mortgage banker's or the investor's interest in income property throughout the term of the loan. Such loans require particular diligence as they may involve significantly large loan balances, intensive management requirements, and complex terms, all of which are susceptible to the changes in business and market conditions. These service procedures require competent handling by trained professionals. Full understanding of all the aspects of income property mortgage financing is a requisite.

Note should also be made of the rapid changes forced from the bottom upward by technology. Much of the appraisal process can now be performed electronically. Borrowers can shop the Internet for rate advantage. Credit information is readily available to all. Title work, insurance, and many other services once controlled by an investor or the lender are but a mouse click away for developers, investors, and lenders, large and small. It may be just beginning. Consider what technology has meant to securitization and commercial mortgage backed securities (CMBS). The rise of the "market servicer" has only been made possible by electronic advancement.

The commercial real estate lending industry is a major player in the financial progress of our nation. It will continue only with the constant training and development of skilled professionals capable of providing the administration and service required in a changing environment. It will not be an easy path you have chosen, but it is rewarding and worthwhile for those with dedication and stamina.

Herbert S. Fecker Jr., CCIM

The Role of Servicing

Upon completion of this chapter, you should be able to

■ ascertain the personnel requirements in mortgage servicing;

■ determine the procedures and training needs of servicing personnel; and

■ distinguish the organizational structures of servicing participants.

■ Introduction

The primary purpose of any servicing organization, whether servicing for its own institution or others, is to protect the investment during the full term of the loan. Income property loans require particular diligence as they involve significantly larger loan balances, intensive management requirements, and complex loan terms, all of which are susceptible to changes in business and market conditions.

The requirements established by the investor in the original loan documents and the general requirements in the overall servicing agreement between investor and correspondent provide the road map that loan administrators must follow in fulfilling their role. A loan administrator must be aware and understand his or her total responsibilities in order to perform the servicing task effectively.

Each member of the servicing team shares the fiduciary responsibility inherent in managing an income property loan. Mortgage payments, escrow accounts, and loan payoffs represent sizable dollars. Sound management and oversight of the receipt, deposit and disbursement of funds by the servicing organization is essential, even when some of these functions may be handled outside the servicing department. This Chapter explores the personnel requirements, training, and structure of a sound commercial real estate servicing department.

■ Personnel Requirements

Managers

Successful servicing managers draw equally on their technical knowledge and their ability to attract, develop, motivate, and direct the members of their servicing team.

Income property loans are varied and complex. Very little can be assumed without reviewing loan documents, analyzing current financial information, or inspecting the property. Managers must have a working knowledge of most, if not all, major aspects of the types of loans being serviced.

Much of the servicing job involves details and priorities. Effective managers are able to delegate responsibility, establish meaningful goals and objectives, communicate well, and follow through to ensure that work quality and accuracy remain high. It is also critical that managers understand and use the many resources available to servicing, including computers, training programs, and special educational materials.

Staff

Most good loan administration people enjoy working with customers and have well-developed "people" skills. Their strengths usually include strong organizational abilities and an orientation toward detail. It is important to remember that service is a major part of what the loan administrator does. Borrowers are customers. They deserve responsiveness, courtesy, and accuracy in their dealings with the servicing organization. Communications with them should be clear and timely.

Basic knowledge about real estate and loan documents (mortgages, notes, assignments, guarantees, leases, deeds, Uniform Commercial Code (UCC) filings, tax bills, and assessments, insurance policies, etc.) and an understanding of loan underwriting, financing terms, income and expense statements, and balance sheets is helpful, if not essential. In addition, loan administration positions generally require some proficiency with computers, numbers, and calculations.

Loan administrators should be familiar with the type of business conducted at each real estate site, understand the problems associated with various income property types, and that the businesses associated with those ventures also differ. Although the servicing staff cannot be expected to have expertise in all these matters, they need to be aware that each type of venture is unique. For example, a loan administrator should be able to recognize that problems related to an apartment complex will differ from those associated with a shopping center. The key to efficient servicing is to know as much as possible about each loan (i.e., market data, type of business conducted, tenants, cash flow, etc.).

■ Servicing Procedures and Training

Servicing procedures for mortgages on income-producing real estate require competent handling by well-trained staff. They should have a background in general servicing, a competent understanding of all aspects of income property mortgage financing, and a thorough working knowledge of the appraisal process, especially as it relates to income property valuation. They need to spend additional time during the training process on underwriting techniques.

A comprehensive, up-to-date operations manual is an invaluable tool for any servicing organization, particularly if team members are inexperienced. While it would be difficult (and not very practical) to include every daily task in the manual, major policies, procedures, and tasks should be defined in writing. This provides consistency in operations and establishes an effective foundation for new employees learning the job.

An ongoing training program is also an essential element in a successful servicing operation. Of course, initial training of new employees is always required. But continuing training is also important to develop new skills and sharpen existing techniques and procedures.

Knowledge of Documentation and Provisions

The servicing function generally begins at the point of funding. As you will learn in Chapter 2, Closing the Loan, the loan administrator, in conjunction with loan underwriters and counsel, must ensure adequate documents and servicing tools are established before funding to provide quality servicing throughout the term of the mortgage.

Once the documentation has been developed, it must be reviewed by the staff and accurate records prepared giving the basic details of the mortgage investment. The loan administrator must be familiar with the supporting documents on income property mortgages so he or she can use the tools provided by this documentation effectively. If there are provisions to help in adverse situations, for instance, or if provisions and documentation call for action by an investor/mortgagee to prevent adverse situations, the loan administrator must know about them.

It may help to have a member of the closing department abstract special provisions and restrictive covenants so they can be reviewed and used by the servicing group. For example, a restrictive covenant may stipulate that the capital of a borrowing entity may not fall below a certain level and that if it does, it triggers a default. In that case, the loan administrator must review the situation annually to avoid a technical default. If default does occur, however, the loan administrator must be prepared to take appropriate action.

The manager of a loan administration/servicing department needs to be involved in evaluating underwriting policy. He or she will then be able to make business officers and attorneys who draft documentation aware of any problems that could be corrected in the future by proper documentation. In this capacity, the manager can also alert the loan administrator to provisions in the mortgage that may require implementation or review in order to comply with the mortgage terms.

Establishing Communications

In addition to the responsibilities involved with the loan documentation, one of the most important servicing functions is establishing effective communications between the mortgagor/borrower and the mortgagee, not only at the beginning of the loan, but throughout the life of the loan. The mortgagor should have a clear understanding of his or her responsibilities in maintaining the mortgage and financial statement requirements, particularly those involving payment, real estate taxes, and insurance. In cases where the loan is being serviced on behalf of the mortgagee, the loan administrator must be identified to the mortgagor well before the first loan payment becomes due and preferably as soon as possible after the loan is funded. Communication between the loan administrator and the investor is also vital to ensure that the loan is serviced according to the investor's requirements.

■ Organizational Structure

Servicing organizations are most often structured in one of two ways:

1. function-based or
2. loan-based.

Both work well, and each has its advantages and disadvantages. The choice depends, for the most part, on the size of the servicing portfolio, the number of investors involved, and the work experience and knowledge of the individual staff members.

Function-Based Organizational Structure

The function-based structure appears to be slightly more prevalent among income property servicing organizations. Individuals are responsible for specific tasks, such as insurance, real estate taxes, payment processing, collections, remittances, inspections/financial statements, etc.

The advantages of this structure include the ability for staffers to develop strong skills and contacts in their specialty. New employees are somewhat easier to train because responsibilities are more narrowly defined.

On the other hand, work is often repetitive and sometimes unrewarding. Work-flow has "peaks and valleys," and cross-training is essential to fill behind absences, vacations, and vacancies. Borrowers must deal with several different staff members during the life of the loan. (On the other hand, these contacts may all be very favorable if each loan administrator is experienced in his or her area of responsibility.)

Loan-Based Organizational Structure

The loan-based structure features Portfolio Managers/Loan Administrators, Account Executives, or Service Specialists who handle most aspects of a selected group of loans. Responsibilities generally include real estate taxes, insurance, financial statements, collections, and most borrower requests.

Loan remittances, payment processing, and loan delinquencies/foreclosures may be handled by function specialists. Portfolio assignments can be made by geographic location, borrower, investor, or a combination of these three. The number of loans assigned to each administrator generally ranges from 75 to 150.

Individual accountability and authority is heightened under this structure. A single contact with the customer (either borrower and/or investor) is possible. Peak workloads are usually balanced among the staff more effectively than in the function-based structure. Flexibility is greater because individuals are able to handle more functions. However, the loan-based structure does require more intensive and thorough training and a higher level of basic skills and abilities.

■ Summary

Servicing income property loans is a demanding business. It requires sound management and business practices and dedicated, hard-working people. A loan administrator must be aware and understand his or her total responsibilities in order to perform the servicing task effectively.

The job begins long before the loan closes. It depends a great deal on effective loan origination and underwriting and comprehensive commitment and closing documents. Lending institutions and mortgage banking organizations have learned to include key loan administrators earlier in the mortgage process to insure that borrower requirements are adequate and clearly stated.

The servicing task is much more difficult if the terms and conditions of the mortgage documents are not understood or improperly identified after the closing occurs. All documents should be reviewed carefully to establish the appropriate procedures and follow-ups necessary to service the loan.

The following Chapters contain invaluable information that will assist the loan administrator in the many functions and activities that are essential in fulfilling his or her responsibilities.

■ Chapter 1 Review Questions

1. Check all of the characteristics of an effective servicing manager.

   _____ Communicates well

   _____ Delegates responsibilities

   _____ Deals effectively and efficiently with borrowers

   _____ Follows through to insure quality and accuracy

2. Servicing staffs are expected to have expertise about the type of business conducted at each real estate site.

   a. True

   b. False

3. At which point does the servicing function generally begin?

   a. Closing

   b. Funding

   c. Origination

   d. Loan Processing

4. Which area requires additional attention by servicing personnel?

   a. Underwriting

   b. Origination

   c. Loan processing

   d. Loan administration

5. Select the two ways that servicing organizations are most often structured.

   _____ Loan-based

   _____ Process-based

   _____ Function-based

   _____ Business-based

6. Which type of organizational structure offers an individual more accountability and authority?

   a. Loan-based

   b. Team-based

   c. Process-based

   d. Function-based

Closing the Loan

learning objectives

Upon completion of this chapter, you should be able to

■ identify the major closing components for a commercial mortgage loan;

■ ascertain borrower closing requirements for a mortgage loan;

■ recognize investor closing needs for a mortgage loan;

■ determine the loan administrator's requirements for closing a mortgage loan; and

■ identify the methods of funding available for mortgage loans.

■ Introduction

The closing function begins when the application/commitment is signed by the investor and borrower and concludes when the mortgage and other loan documents are recorded and the loan proceeds are disbursed from the investor. Between these two events the loan must be documented and all business and due diligence items must be completed.

Though most documents, procedures, and provisions are standardized in many respects, the preparation of loan documents and pre-closing procedures should never be viewed as standardized. Each loan transaction has its own nuances, and lenders have their own closing procedures, all of which need to be appropriately addressed.

Proper guidance and involvement by the lender's legal counsel and careful coordination with the lender's closing and/or legal departments are imperative. This Chapter details the significant documentation in a closing file, the closing procedures of borrowers, investors, and loan administrators, and the methods of funding commercial loans.

■ The Closing

Notification to Involved Parties

All parties to the closing should be given the name of the staff member at the loan administrator's office who will coordinate the closing, and they should be requested to direct all correspondence regarding the file to that person's attention. Conversely, the loan administrator should determine who at the investor's and borrower's offices will be handling the closing from both business and legal standpoints. The title company contact should also be distributed to borrower and investor.

Closing Delays and Extensions

If it appears that all the commitment requirements will not be met by the stated closing date, an extension should be requested from the investor in writing. (Don't forget to extend the maturity of any standby letters of credit or certificates of deposit.) In the event of a construction loan with an interim and permanent investor, it is particularly important that a request for delay in permanent funding be anticipated as far in advance as possible.

■ Commitment Letter

A closing file should be prepared upon receipt of a fully accepted and executed commitment letter. The commitment letter outlines all the conditions that must be accomplished before the loan can be closed and the documents recorded. This closing file should include a copy of the commitment letter and copies of any amendments to the commitment letter. Expiration dates of the commitment and any standby letters of credit should be noted for follow-up.

Whether dealing with a commitment between the borrower and investor, or a buy-sell agreement (an agreement entered into by an interim and a permanent investor for the sale and assignment of the mortgage to the permanent investor when construction is completed), there are numerous business decisions to be made. Generally, the decision process will be completed by the investor's underwriter, with input from the loan administrator.

The loan administrator must be fully conversant with the closing requirements of the commitment letter. It is not enough for the loan administrator to act merely as a conduit for information, documents, and exhibits. The loan administrator must be aware of the investor's requirements and knowledgeable about the documents securing the investment so that the administration can expedite both documentation and due diligence items and anticipate where problems may arise that will require a negotiated settlement.

Servicing/Correspondent Agreement

The servicing or correspondent agreement is a bilateral agreement between the correspondent and investor that governs the business relationship. The agreement sets forth the servicing functions and duties that are to be performed in return for specific consideration. The agreement may also refer to loan origination, defining the correspondent's territory, or detailing the handling of co-brokered loans and referrals. Agreements differ greatly between investors.

Some are very vague and poorly written while others are very specific and include a variety of helpful exhibits.

Servicing manual   A servicing or correspondent agreement should be all-inclusive, covering every servicing situation which may arise. However, due to the evolving nature of the servicing industry, many agreements are quickly outdated or may not cover a specific situation. Some investors handle this problem by stating in the agreement that the correspondent will perform his or her duties according to a servicing manual that may be attached as an exhibit to the agreement. The servicing manual outlines the investor's specific procedures for the loan administrator to follow.

If a manual is not available from the investor, a file of correspondence relating to procedures should be maintained for reference. All verbal changes to pre-established procedures should be confirmed in writing and updated in the manual or file. If there is a question about how the investor wants a specific item handled, clarification should be requested.

■ Loan Documents

The loan documents describe the legal rights of the parties' investor and borrower requirements and establish in legal forms the requirements in the commitment. They include the promissory note and mortgage or deed of trust.

Normally, the permanent investors will want to have their attorney prepare the mortgage documents. The loan administrator can be of valuable assistance in this process by knowing the investor's escrow requirements and type of forms needed. For example, an investor may have standard forms of survey requirements, architect's certification, tenant estoppel and subordination, nondisturbance and attornment agreement (SNDA). The loan administrator should have all these standard forms on file and provide copies as necessary to the borrower.

If you service loans, you must familiarize yourself with the requirements that are set forth in the loan documents. Today's technology allows you to track much of this information through computers. First, however, you must be able to locate the pertinent information in each loan document and then input this information into your mortgage servicing system. A more in-depth discussion of each loan document follows.

Promissory Note

The promissory note evidences the borrower's promise to pay the loan. Among other things, the note reflects the original principal amount of the loan, the interest rate(s), the terms of the payment of principal and interest, and the maturity date. Legal counsel should ensure that other elements and language are contained in the note to adequately protect the lender. Counsel should also ensure that the note is a negotiable instrument under the Uniform Commercial Code (UCC) in those jurisdictions where the code has been adopted. The note references the mortgage or deed of trust that secures the note and frequently incorporates its terms. At a minimum, the note should reflect that a default under the mortgage/deed of trust will constitute a default under the note. In fact, the note should be cross-defaulted with all other documents evidencing the loan.

Provisions/Clauses   *Prepayment Terms.* Not all loans are prepayable. If prepayment is allowed, the lender may dictate when the note may be prepaid. Furthermore, the lender can require the payment of a prepayment or penalty fee. This fee is calculated by measuring the lost economic opportunity to the lender had the loan been repaid over the entire scheduled term.

Cure Periods and Notice Requirements. The existence and length of cure periods for defaults and whether notice of defaults must be given to the borrower are not automatic. Different provisions for cures and notice are often negotiated based upon whether the default is monetary (such as the payment of a principal and interest installment) or nonmonetary (such as repairing damage to the property).

Default Provisions. The note must include the events which will cause the note to be in default. Each event need not be specifically identified in the note (other than, perhaps, the failure to pay principal and interest installments on time). Although, a reference to make timely payments comply with the terms and provisions of all the documents evidencing the loan is common.

Acceleration of Maturity. Hand-in-hand with the default provision is the acceleration of maturity provision, without which the ability to foreclose or to exercise the power of sale could be fatal.

Late Charges and Default Rate of Interest. These amounts are often negotiated, but, in any event, must be limited by the maximum rate of interest permitted under applicable law.

Joint and Several Liability. This provision is always appropriate, even when there is only one borrower at loan inception. This protects the lender in the event that the loan is modified at post-closing to add additional borrowers.

Usury. A so-called usury savings clause should appear in every note. The laws of the governing jurisdiction must be carefully examined by legal counsel in order to incorporate the appropriate usury savings clause.

Recourse versus Non-recourse Loans. In most jurisdictions, unless otherwise indicated in the loan documents, the note is recourse, which means that the borrower(s) is personally liable for the repayment of the debt. If the loan is non-recourse, the lender will want to exclude certain matters from the general effect of the non-recourse language, such as, liability for environmental contamination, failure to pay taxes and insurance premiums, and retention of rental income after a default.

Waiver of Trial by Jury Provision. In many jurisdictions, such a provision has been deemed enforceable. Its inclusion is generally beneficial to the lender.

Mortgage or Deed of Trust

The mortgage/deed of trust evidences the real property collateral for the repayment of the promissory note. Once properly recorded, the mortgage/deed of trust establishes a lien on the real estate encumbered thereby with a priority position that will be insured by the title insurance policy. The following provisions are commonly found in most mortgages/deeds of trust:

Description of the Encumbered Property. Not only should the real property be specifically described by a legal description (which should be identical to the legal descriptions contained in the survey and the title insurance policy), but all other property (personal and intangible property) in which the lender desires a security interest should be described in great detail. If the borrower does not execute a separate security agreement, the mortgage or deed of trust should include a section containing a grant of a security interest in the non-real estate collateral, as well as provisions governing the lender's remedies regarding such collateral.

Due-on-Sale and Encumbrance Clauses. A properly drafted due-on-sale clause should address a sale or transfer of the encumbered property (or any part thereof) and also a sale or transfer of any (or some minimum level of) interest in the borrower.

Depending upon the terms of the loan, the lender may wish to incorporate a provision allowing the sale of the encumbered property without invoking the due-on-sale clause and providing for the assumption of the loan. The terms of assumption must be clearly set forth. Such terms commonly include a requirement that the transferee be "creditworthy," execute an assumption agreement, and pay an assumption fee and any other charges associated therewith.

The mortgage/deed of trust should also provide for the ability to accelerate the loan in the event subordinate liens are filed against the property, such as a second mortgage, judgments, or mechanic's liens. In the event secondary financing is permitted, the specific terms of such financing must be incorporated into the mortgage or deed of trust. These terms frequently include the maximum amount of permitted secondary financing and the requirement for a subordination agreement from the subordinate lender in form and substance satisfactory to the prior lender. The maximum amount of secondary financing is often tied to the available cash flow from the property or is a percentage of the value of the encumbered property.

Insurance Provisions/Premiums. The borrower must keep current the payment of all insurance premiums for required policies under the mortgage or deed of trust and provide timely proof of such payment to the lender. Typical insurance policies include hazard, liability, business interruption, earthquake, and automobile. The delivery of proof of payment must be early enough so that if such proof is not delivered, the lender will have sufficient time to pay the insurance before policies lapse. The lender must be entitled under the mortgage or deed of trust to advance monies to pay premiums, which amounts will then be secured. All policies should name the lender as an additional insured and/or reflect the lender as a mortgagee. Each policy should also provide that it may not be terminated, amended, or modified except after 30 days prior notice to the lender, and that prior notice will be given to the lender in the event the policy is not renewed.

Real Estate Taxes. The borrower must promptly pay real estate taxes and provide the lender with proof of such payment. Many lenders require that taxes and charges such as special assessments be paid no later than the date on which they become delinquent. In jurisdictions where a property owner is entitled to a discount if taxes are paid early, lenders may require that taxes be paid by a date that will entitle the borrower to the maximum available discount. Accommodations are often made to allow the borrower to contest the tax amount or property assessment. In these instances, sufficient safeguards must be incorporated to ensure that, at no time during the context process, may the taxing authorities be capable of levying against the property or selling the property at a tax sale for the continuing failure to pay taxes. The mortgage or deed of trust must permit the lender to advance monies under the mortgage or deed of trust upon the failure of the borrower to timely pay the taxes.

Insurance and Real Estate Tax Escrows. Provisions providing for escrows are the best means of ensuring the timely payment of real estate taxes and insurance premiums. Escrows enable the lender to accumulate amounts for taxes and premiums before they become due and payable. In the event a default occurs, the lender will have monies available to offset the amounts due without having to advance the full amount. Many borrowers prefer not to establish escrows. They prefer to have escrows required only in the event of a default. Borrowers also will seek to have all escrowed money placed in an interest-bearing account.

■ Closing Requirements

Closing requirements are outlined specifically in the permanent loan commitment and must be received and approved prior to the loan closing. Mortgage loan checklists ensure that the requirements of borrowers, investors, and loan administrators are covered. Figure 2.1 is an example of a borrower checklist, Figure 2.2 is for an investor, and Figure 2.3 shows the closing mechanics.

■ Methods of Funding Loans

The loan administrator should coordinate between investor and borrower the method of funding. Following are standard methods of transferring funds.

Wire Transfer of Funds

This method is used by most investors to transfer large amounts of money quickly. Investors authorize their banks to transfer loan proceeds by federal funds to the bank of either the borrower, the construction investor, or the title/escrow company.

To avoid problems, those responsible for implementing the wire transfer should give specific instructions and make sure the transferring bank has the correct information. Delays can be costly, because interest charges on the amount usually begin at the time of transfer. To avoid problems, the loan administrator should provide the investor with the following information:

■ Name and address of the receiving bank, including ABA number
■ Officer contact name and telephone number at the bank
■ Account name and number with contact name at the title company or loan administrator's office

When funds have been wired, the loan administrator should obtain the wire reference number and time the funds went on the wire and pass the information to the receiving party to help expedite prompt credit of funds.

Figure 2.1 | Borrower Responsibilities

Business Requirements

- Commitment—accepted by borrower (the loan administrator should review for any unusual servicing requirements)
- Fees
  - Commitment fee (refundable and/or nonrefundable)
  - Underwriting fee (if any)
  - Site inspection fee
  - Architectural fees
- As-built plans and specifications including all addenda, field orders, and change orders
- Soil report
- Flood map
- Phase I environmental site assessment
- Architectural/engineering survey (including seismic review if required)
- Borrower's financial statements
- Borrower's credit reports
- Standard form lease
- Tenant documentation (include for each tenant)
  - Lease (leases should be reviewed to be certain the economics of the lease correspond to the loan underwritten by the investor)
  - Estoppel on investor's standard form
  - Subordination and attornment agreement (if required) and including nondisturbance, if allowed (investor's standard form)
  - Certificate of occupancy
  - Financial statements (if required)
  - Retail credit report (if required)
  - Any lease guaranties
- Certified rent roll
- 8" x 10" photographs of the property (interior and exterior)
- Inventory of personal property
- List of any service contracts (i.e., elevator, maintenance)
- Certificate of cost
- Letter of credit (if required)
- M.A.I. appraisal
- Life insurance for designated persons (if required)
- Additional items if newly constructed property:
  - Certificate of substantial completion
  - Notice(s) of completion
  - Roofing certificate
  - Copies of construction contracts/warranties, or guarantees which give ongoing protection

Figure 2.1 | Borrower Responsibilities *(Continued)*

- Additional items if construction loan:
    - Construction contracts
        - General contractor
        - Architect
        - Engineer
        - Major subcontractors
- Bonds, if required
- Draw request format (review to be certain the requirements are clear)
- Copies of building permits
- Evidence of zoning, subdivision, building laws, and any other governmental approvals
- Plans and specifications
- Utility letters (verification of availability)
- Development budget (with architect's approval)

Authorization/Legal Documents

- Corporation
    - Articles of incorporation
    - Bylaws
    - Certificate of good standing from Secretary of State
    - Resolution from Board authorizing borrowing
    - Franchise tax certificate
    - Incumbency certificate
    - Current financial statements
- Partnership
    - Partnership agreement (certified by General Partner)
    - Certificate of limited partnership (LP-1)
    - Certificate of good standing from Secretary of State
    - Partnership authorization for borrowing (unless covered in partnership agreement)
    - Fictitious business name statements (with proof of publication)
    - Current financial statements
- Trust indenture
- Borrower's counsel's opinion (form to be provided by investor's counsel)
- Tax identification number for borrower

Figure 2.1 | Borrower Responsibilities *(Continued)*

Real Estate Documents

- Title insurance
  - Commitment (or preliminary title report) with copies of all back-up documents listed
  - Pro forma (sample of how final form will appear)
  - Title policy (issued at closing)
- Copy of grant deed
- Copy of any reciprocal easement agreement (REA) or covenants, conditions, and restrictions (CC&Rs)
- Current survey in accordance with investor's requirements
  - Preliminary (if construction loan)
  - As-built
- Insurance
  - Hazard and casualty
  - Builders risk (if construction loan)
  - Rent and/or business interruption
  - Flood (if property is shown in an "A" zone on the flood map)
  - Earthquake, if required
  - Boiler and machinery, if applicable
  - General and excess liability coverage
- Completion certificates (for construction loan)
  - Borrower
  - Loan administrator
  - Borrower's architect
- Governmental approvals
  - Certificate of occupancy for building
- For hospital/nursing home
  - License
  - Medicare/Medicaid certification
  - Certificate of need
  - Hospital accreditation
  - Certification that construction complies with Medicare/Medicaid requirement
- For hotel/restaurant
  - Liquor license
  - Health Department certification (if required)
- Environmental certification
- Zoning approval
- Real property tax bills for current year
- Tax service contract (obtained at closing) (upon receipt, review to be certain legal description is accurate)

Figure 2.2 | Investor Responsibilities

Documents to be prepared by investor's counsel or investor's outside counsel.

- Participation agreement
- Triparty/buy-sell agreement (between construction investor, permanent investor, and borrower). Review to be certain the document is specific about what items will be required before the permanent investor takes loan.
- Escrow agreement for any holdback (if required)
- For tax-exempt mortgage loan closings
  - Inducement bond resolution
  - Bond resolution or ordinance
  - Bond
  - Transfer of bond (interim investor to permanent investor)
  - Loan agreement
  - UCC statements for loan agreement
  - Pledge of loan agreement
  - Assignment of pledge (interim investor to permanent investor)
  - Bond counsel's opinion
  - Holdback escrow agreement
  - Trust indenture
- Promissory note (Loan administrator should review for collection problems. Do payment terms make sense? Is maturity date clear? Review late charge provision and prepayment provisions.)
- Guaranty(ies)
- Mortgage (deed of trust) and security agreement (loan administrator should review sections on insurance, annual reports, lease requirements; impounds; any holdback provisions and late charges to be certain they are clear.)
- UCC financing statements (loan administrator should be certain to obtain filing information after closing in order to file continuation statements)
- UCC-3 search
- Assignment of rents, leases, and other benefits such as construction guarantees
- Borrower's certificate
- Estoppel certificate from any third parties such as parties to REA, CC&Rs, or redevelopment authority
- Assignment of security documents
  - Endorsement of note
  - Assignment of mortgage (deed of trust)
  - Assignment of
    - Leases
    - Rents
    - Architects/contractors agreements (for construction loan)
    - Management agreement (and consent of manager, if applicable)
    - UCCs (for construction loan)

Figure 2.2 | Investor Responsibilities *(Continued)*

- Special counsel's opinion
- Assignment and recognition agreement for furniture/equipment leases
- Letter of credit or holdback agreements (if required)
- Franchise/license agreement
- Recognition agreements (or estoppels)
  - Ground leases
  - Franchisor/licensor
- Inspecting architect (for construction loans)
  - Selection
  - Reports
  - Completion certificate
- Site inspection
- Environmental indemnity

Figure 2.3 | Closing Mechanics

- Closing protection letter from title insurance company (insured closing)
- Escrows or letters of credit and holdback agreements for the following:
  - Taxes and insurance
  - Completion
  - Rent-up
  - Operating income shortfall
- Interest in advance at closing (if required)
- Tax and insurance premium adjustments (if any)
- Fees
  - Investor and/or special counsel fees
  - Bond counsel's fees
  - Trustee's fees
  - Custodial fees
  - Loan origination and/or broker fees
  - Architects' fees
  - Tax service fee (if required by loan administrator)
- Wiring instructions (obtain from the title or escrow company and provide to investor) at least 48 hours before funding. Borrower should also provide title or escrow company with wiring instructions for any excess loan proceeds.
- Recording instructions to title company/escrow agent
- Closing statement from escrow or title company
  - Pre-closing statement lists anticipated closing costs
  - Post-closing statement gives accurate accounting of all monies received and disbursed
- Post-closing return of commitment fees, architectural fees, or letters of credit

Check

There are two types of checks that can be used to transfer funds for a loan closing. One is a federal funds check and the other is a clearinghouse check. A federal funds check is drawn on the Federal Reserve Bank in the district and represents good funds available on the day the check is drawn and delivered. A clearinghouse check can be issued by the investor or by a bank or cashier's check drawn on the investor's bank.

■ Loan Setup after Closing

If the loan administrator has been involved in the closing or has had an opportunity to review the loan documents, it should be clear which items need to be set up for follow-up. These would include insurance, taxes, inspections, leases, UCC continuations, annual financial reports, and any holdback provisions or post-closing items.

Sub-Files

Sub-files are recommended over a master file because of the advantage of being able to go to a specific file without searching through the master file. If a master file is necessary, copying specific pages from the documents and placing them in sub-files is a good idea.

Review Documents

It is imperative that all documents securing the investment be thoroughly analyzed and the information prepared for entry into a computer or manual system. The entries would include billing information such as the interest rate, mortgage term, late charges, additional interest, and any escrows. All follow-up dates should be entered into the system for items such as UCC continuations, financial statements, taxes, insurance, and note expiration. Audit controls must be in place to determine the accuracy of the information.

Insurance

The loan administrator must be sure that tax and insurance premium payments are thoroughly understood and are properly adjusted and funded at closing and reviewed at loan setup.

Communicate with the Mortgagor

After the documents are analyzed, the loan administrator should explain the billing method to the mortgagor by letter. The letter should state the name and telephone number of the administrator to be contacted for assistance. It is wise to outline in this letter any procedures that the mortgagor should follow such as the submittal of leases for review, annual financial statements, etc.

■ Summary

This Chapter looked at the components of a closing file, the responsibilities of the parties involved in a closing, the methods of funding loans, and the loan setup after closing has taken place. The main components of a closing file include the commitment letter, loan documents, servicing or correspondent agreement, and servicing manual. The loan administrator must notify parties of closing activities and any closing delays.

The most common methods of funding mortgage loans include wire transfer of funds and check submission. After funds have been disbursed at closing, loan administrators continue to follow up on the loan. They insure that insurance, taxes, inspections, licenses, UCC continuations, financial reports, and hold provisions are current.

■ Chapter 2 Review Questions

1. Who normally prepares the mortgage documents?
   a. Interim investor's attorney
   b. Permanent investor's attorney
   c. Closing agent
   d. Title company

2. Verbal changes to pre-established procedures in a servicing manual must be confirmed in writing.
   a. True
   b. False

3. Which type of fee is *NOT* a requirement of the borrower?
   a. Estoppel
   b. Commitment
   c. Architectural
   d. Underwriting
   e. Site inspection

4. Which item may be required of a borrower who has newly constructed property?
   a. Termite inspection
   b. Roofing certificate
   c. Holdback agreement
   d. Bond counsel's opinion

5. For tax exempt mortgage loans, investors may need to provide all of the following *EXCEPT*
   a. assignment of pledge.
   b. environmental indemnity.
   c. bond resolution or ordinance.
   d. UCC statements for a loan agreement.

6. Prior to closing, who is responsible for providing a tri-party agreement among a borrower, a construction lender, and a permanent lender?
   a. Investor
   b. Borrower
   c. Attorney-in-fact
   d. Loan administrator

7. A loan administrator must provide wiring instructions to an investor at least how long before funding?
   a. 24 hours
   b. 48 hours
   c. 72 hours
   d. 5 days

8. Due to the evolving nature of the servicing industry, servicing agreements are quickly outdated.
   a. True
   b. False

9. Check the two standard methods of transferring loan funds.
   _____ Check
   _____ Certified check
   _____ Wire transfer
   _____ Automatic withdrawal

10. Which type of check is drawn on the Federal Reserve Bank in the district and represents "good funds" available on the day the check is drawn and delivered?
    a. Insured
    b. Federal
    c. Government
    d. Clearinghouse

Payment Processing

learning objectives

Upon completion of this chapter, you should be able to

- identify the components in the loan billing process;

- recognize the delinquent collection procedures for loans;

- distinguish the action steps in the loan collection process; and

- ascertain the steps in processing cash received for loans.

■ Introduction

The collection of payments is one of the primary responsibilities of the mortgage loan administrator. Establishing effective collection procedures begins immediately after loan closing with the administrator's first written contact with the borrower. This initial "hello" letter communicates the amount of the first payment, the due date, and the charges assessed if the payment is late. This letter also explains if monthly or coupon book billing will be instituted. Finally, this correspondence requests the name, address, and telephone number of the person who will be responsible for the loan.

The use of a coupon book or direct billing creates regular communication between the loan administrator and borrower. If payment guidelines are not followed, the administrator may need to institute delinquent collection procedures. These procedures include late charges, default rates, acceleration, and assignment of rents. If these measures fail, foreclosure may become the only remaining solution.

■ Billing Process

The billing process creates a regular communication between the loan administrator and borrower and is typically accomplished by either coupon book or direct billing. If the payment is fixed or level, the loan administrator may elect to provide a coupon book. However, if the payment is based on a changing interest rate or other varying loan terms, a direct billing may be necessitated based on the payment frequency required in the note. In either method, the information provided may include such items as the total payment due, the date after which the payment will be considered late, the amount of late charge, the amount of escrows, and possibly the remaining principal balance after payment is made.

■ Delinquent Collection Procedures

Although computer-generated reminder notices or form letters requesting overdue payments are generally issued, these should be immediately followed by telephone contact with the person responsible for making the mortgage payment. This call should be positive, but firm, and remind the borrower that if payment is not received before the end of any "grace period," a late charge will be assessed. Assessing a late charge on the first instance of a late payment will communicate a firm policy.

Once a payment becomes late, the loan administrator should contact the borrower by telephone to determine when the delinquent payment can be expected and the reason or cause for the delinquency. The loan administrator should also contact the investor to advise of the late payment and when payment can be expected. If the borrower does not remit the payment, then immediately, or at least prior to the due date of the next installment due, the loan administrator shall draft and deliver, by means of certified mail, an appropriate notice of formal demand for payment and forward a copy to the investor.

The sending of a formal demand letter or any other actions should be dictated by the investor and be in accordance with the provisions of the loan documents. If a loan becomes 30 days delinquent, the loan administrator may want to initiate other actions to ensure the security of the investor is being maintained. These actions may include a physical inspection of the real estate, obtaining operating statements and a current rent roll, and a recommendation to the investor in writing of an appropriate course of action.

Late Charges

A late charge is an effective collection tool that is used to encourage prompt payment and also offsets the expense incurred in collection of the payment. Income property mortgages frequently provide for a late fee in the form of a percentage of the payment or as additional interest on the installments. The note dictates the charge percent for late fees. As payments on income property mortgages involve substantial amounts, the late fee assessment will be of concern to the borrower, and it is meant to have that effect. Collectors should use the late fee when it is justified. If the delinquency is caused by circumstances beyond the borrower's control, imposing a late charge may add a financial burden and create a more serious default. In addition, because the laws in some states prohibit the use of a late charge, loan administrators should be thoroughly familiar with the state requirements in their servicing area before assessing a late charge. Loan administrators should never waive late charges without the knowledge and consent of the investor.

Default Rate

Commercial mortgages generally provide for a default rate. The time frame and amount of the default rate will be covered in the loan documents. Some mortgages provide for automatic imposition of a default rate; others require that a notice of default allowing for a cure period be sent to the borrower. If the latter is the case, it is important that proper notice be sent. Some states have specific regulations dealing with default situations and the imposition of the default rate may put the mortgage in a usurious condition. Assuming that documents were reviewed by local counsel when the mortgage was created, there may be subsequent changes to the usury law, which should be checked by the loan administrator prior to instituting the default rate. Also, the investor should be consulted. If the default rate is instituted, the loan administrator should advise the borrower in writing that the default rate is in effect. It is important to communicate with the borrower as often as possible to encourage the default to be cured.

Acceleration

Many mortgages provide for an acceleration clause indicating that if the loan is in default, it may be accelerated and payment of the total mortgage amount required. The mention of the possibility of acceleration will heighten the awareness of the borrower to the investor's insistence on timely payment.

Assignment of Rents

As additional collateral, many mortgage documents provide for the assignment of rents on income properties and the appointment of a receiver. Assignment of rents many times requires court approval, so it is vital to check with local counsel. The appointment of a receiver and the assignment of rents may be the first visible sign to the borrower's tenants that there may be financial problems. Under the assignment of rents, the borrower's tenants would receive notice that they are to make their lease payments into an escrow account. Because assignment of rents may embarrass the borrower, the suggestion of its use can be effective. By exercising the assignment of rents, the loan administrator and investor must also be prepared to take on any engagement responsibility, because operating expenses will need to be paid.

Foreclosure

After all other collection alternatives have been considered and determined to be ineffective, discuss foreclosure with the borrower. Sometimes the likelihood of foreclosure is enough to establish a communication that will lead to a collection plan, short of requiring court supervision. Foreclosure is a valid collection tool, but it can be a long and tedious process and should be used as a last resort.

■ Collection Process Checklists

The following checklists include some of the actions the loan administrator should take throughout the collection process.

Collection Calls

- Phone each delinquent account within five days of the delinquency date on the loan. (If no grace period is provided for in the loan documents, this phone call should be made prior to close of business on the payment due date.)
- Determine reason for delinquency and when payment can be expected.

- If verbal attempts at collection are unsuccessful, a written demand letter should be sent to the borrower via certified mail, return receipt requested. A copy should be sent to the lender.
- Document each contact attempt manually and/or on the company system.
- Follow up delinquent accounts to insure the borrower performs as promised.
- Notify the lender immediately both verbally and in writing.
- Provide property information as requested by the lender and make recommendations as necessary on those accounts that may require a workout.

Notices and Letters

- Mail reminder notices within ten days of the due date.
- Mail late charge notices on date late charge is assessed.
- Prepare and mail demand letters as instructed by the lender. Normally these letters would be sent between the 15th and 30th day of delinquency.

Late Charges/Partial Payments

- Monitor the collection of late charges to help defray the administrative costs of additional collection efforts.
- Partial payments (including payments received without the late charge) should not be accepted without the consent of the lender.

Reports

- Prepare monthly delinquency reports as required by the lender, noting the amount past due and the reason for the delinquency.
- Complete the monthly summary of delinquent loans for internal management, if required.

■ Processing Cash

Processing cash is a vital function that requires maximum efficiency to ensure that all cash is processed in the most expedient manner. It is critical that all lenders receive their remittances at the earliest possible date. It is also crucial that this function be established with audit guidelines.

Payments must be processed daily and will normally utilize one of the following methods:

1. Direct payment
2. Lock box
3. Bank wires
4. Automated Clearing House (ACH)

After receipt of the payment through one of the above methods, processing procedures occur as follows:

- Verify the payment amount to ensure that it is correct for the amount of the monthly payment(s) or, in the case of a payoff, for the full amount due. Also verify the payee and date of the check.

- Monitor the various hold codes on your computer system to ensure that there are no "stops." Stops may include matured loans, no personal checks, or other defaults that may require special handling.
- Refer any deficiency payments or payments with "hold" codes to the collector, management, or lender for further information.
- Return any payment to borrower only when specifically instructed by the lender.
- Advise the borrower of any shortages (only after the lender instructs servicer to accept short payment).
- Balance all cash receipts to transactions processed. Endorse all checks as required and prepare deposit slips.

The loan administrator should deposit all principal and interest funds received from the borrower(s) in a custodial demand account. This account must be separate from the servicer's funds or other collection funds and deposited with a bank acceptable to the lender.

The custodial demand account should be styled as follows (or as otherwise directed by each individual lender): "John Smith Mortgage Company as Servicer for A-1 Life Insurance Company." Loan administrators should remit the funds from the borrower(s) less the amount of their servicing fees directly to the lenders or their designees. These funds may be remitted by one of the previously described methods (as required by each individual lender). The servicer should request necessary remittance instructions for each lender and maintain these records on file. The loan administrator should send the lender a mortgage loan collection (or remittance) report detailing the respective funds sent to the lender in a form approved by the lender. Many lenders are now requiring this report be sent by facsimile.

■ Summary

This Chapter covered the importance of the collection and processing of mortgage loan payments. By establishing consistent collection practices and procedures, loan administrators can reduce the number of delinquent accounts.

It is necessary to contact the borrower immediately after loan closing to communicate the necessary payment information. The use of coupon books or direct billing methods encourages regular communication between the loan administrator and borrower. If payments become late, delinquent collection procedures in the form of late charges, default rates, acceleration, and assignment of rents may be instituted. Should these alternatives fail, foreclosure proceedings may be necessary.

Checklists that provide useful reminders of actions the loan administrator needs to take during the collection process were covered. Finally, the process involved in handling cash remittances was addressed.

■ Chapter 3 Review Questions

1. Check the two ways borrowers are typically billed for mortgage loans.

   _____ Direct billing

   _____ Coupon book

   _____ Electronic debit

   _____ Automatic withdrawal

2. The direct billing method is used for loans whose payment is based on a

   a. fixed interest rate.

   b. changing interest rate.

   c. 15-year adjustable-rate mortgage.

   d. 30-year conventional mortgage.

3. Which mortgage frequently provides for a late fee that is a percentage of the payment or as additional interest on the installments?

   a. Wraparound

   b. Residential

   c. Adjustable rate

   d. Income property

4. Under an assignment of rents, a borrower's tenants would make lease payments

   a. directly to a trustee.

   b. into an escrow account.

   c. directly to the borrower.

   d. into a reserve funds account.

5. All of the following items may be on a collection call checklist *EXCEPT*

   a. notify the lender immediately both verbally and in writing.

   b. determine the reason for the delinquency and when payment can be expected.

   c. document each contact attempt manually and/or on the computer.

   d. provide information as requested by the lender and solicit recommendations from the borrower to complete a workout.

6. Partial payments from a borrower can be accepted without the consent of the lender.

   a. True

   b. False

7. Which is *NOT* a method of processing mortgage payments?

   a. Lock box

   b. Bank wires

   c. Western Union

   d. Automatic Clearing House

8. Loan administrators deposit all principal and interest funds received from borrowers in a

   a. demand depository.

   b. remittance account.

   c. custodial depository.

   d. custodial demand account

Escrow Analysis

learning objectives

Upon completion of this chapter, you should be able to

- identify the escrow considerations employed by loan administrators;

- ascertain the types of insurance coverage for income properties;

- recognize the main clauses and endorsements in mortgage insurance policies;

- discern the common insurance loss settlement procedures;

- determine the environmental issues affecting mortgage lenders; and

- identify the tax and municipal assessment considerations for income properties.

■ Introduction

The documentation for many income property mortgages requires that an escrow deposit account be established to accumulate funds for payment of real estate taxes, special assessments on the mortgaged property, premiums for hazard insurance coverage, and mortgage insurance premiums, when required. Such funds are held in escrow for payment of these accruing obligations.

Loan administrators determine the amount of the monthly escrow deposit to be paid by the mortgagor based on a regular analysis of bills to be paid. This lesson reviews each component of an escrow deposit account, with particular attention paid to hazard insurance coverage.

■ Escrow Overview

Except where prohibited by law, or where otherwise agreed to in writing by the investor, the mortgagor must deposit enough money in an escrow account each month to pay the estimated insurance premiums, taxes, ground rents, special assessments, and other charges as they become due and payable. These items are paid from the mortgagor's or borrower's escrow account, but if the funds are insufficient, a situation primarily caused by increases in the tax bills, it is necessary to collect the deficiency from the mortgagor and to adjust the mortgagor's payments for the future based on the increased amounts. The investor and/or the loan administrator (at the investor's direction) may choose either to advance the funds when a deficiency occurs, to pay the bills and collect the advance, or to wait until the deficiency has been paid by the mortgagor before paying the bills.

■ Escrow Guidelines

Responsibility of Loan Administrator

Loan administrators are responsible for the administration of the mortgagor's escrow account. They determine the amount of the monthly escrow deposit to be paid by the mortgagor based on a regular analysis of bills to be paid. An escrow account should be analyzed every time funds are disbursed, but at least annually. More frequent analysis is prudent to prevent a deficiency and because bills received for payment, especially for real estate taxes, may have increased substantially.

The results of the analysis should be furnished to the mortgagor and to the investor, if they wish to be kept informed of such matters. The loan administrator must also assure the timely payment of taxes, assessments, hazard insurance, and mortgage insurance premiums to avoid penalties and to take advantage of any discounts offered.

An investor may waive an escrow account in total or for specific escrow items, such as hazard insurance, even though the documentation provides for their collection. Many times in granting a waiver, it will be conditioned so that should the mortgagor fail to pay the items or the loan goes into default for another reason, the escrow account may be reactivated. Extreme caution should be taken in waiving escrow deposits. Even though the loan documents may require escrow deposits, once they have been waived, it can be very difficult to get the mortgagor to begin making deposits, even if an event of default has taken place.

The loan administrator should, and in some states must, provide the mortgagor with an annual statement of the mortgagor's escrow account, setting forth in summary form the balance of the account at the beginning of the year, the total amount deposited into the account by the mortgagor during the year, the amount, date, and nature of any disbursements made from the account during the year, and the final balance at the end of the year. In addition, the loan administrator should provide the mortgagor with a statement at calendar year-end as to the interest and taxes paid by the mortgagor during the year. Copies of these should also be forwarded to the investor, if requested.

Escrows for Second Mortgages and Wraparounds

Mortgagees are obligated to maintain current insurance and pay taxes when they are due. Whether in a second mortgage position or with a wraparound loan, the mortgagee must consider the requirements of the first mortgagee. In some cases, a tax and insurance escrow may be required; in others, only one of the two is necessary.

If loan administrators are not maintaining the escrows, they need to verify that insurance is current and taxes are paid. One way of doing this is to collect the payments for insurance and taxes even though they are passed through to the underlying mortgagee. If payments are made directly to the first mortgagee, then a good relationship with that investor often will result in prompt verification of payments.

Surplus

Where the loan administrator determines that a surplus exists in a mortgagor's escrow account, refunds to the mortgagor may be made, provided that the mortgage is current, and that other nonmonetary defaults do not exist. Alternatively, any excess may be considered in fixing the amount of the deposit for the following year. When the surplus is sufficient or is supplemented by an additional collection, it may be applied to one or more installment payments of principal and interest, or as an additional principal payment, provided such actions are consistent with the terms of the mortgage instrument and the wishes of the mortgagor and investor.

Deficiencies

When the loan administrator determines that a deficit exists in an escrow account, it is customary in servicing income property mortgages to require that a deficiency be paid as quickly as possible. Depending on investor requirements, arrangements may be made to permit repayment of the deficit over a specific time period rather than in a lump sum, especially if the amount of the deficiency is substantial.

Trends

A well-managed mortgage company should maintain trend records showing real estate tax and/or insurance premium adjustments, as this information will help in future escrow analysis. Automated programs can be developed for tracking the information using computers.

■ Insurance Requirements

One of the most important responsibilities of the income property loan administrator is to ensure that proper and adequate insurance is secured and maintained on all properties in the portfolio. This task is also one of the most difficult because of the complexity of insurance policies and the variance in requirements from one mortgagee to the next. Some investors establish quite specific criteria for acceptable insurance coverage and some merely state that insurance must be furnished in amounts and coverage satisfactory to the investor.

The borrower must maintain proper fire and extended coverage hazard insurance in accordance with the requirements set forth in the loan documents. All original policies are to be retained by servicers (unless otherwise directed by lender) and endorsed in favor of lenders as their interest may appear. A tickler file of expiration dates of all policies should be maintained by servicers to avoid policy lapses. Certified copies of the policy or other evidence of insurance should be accepted only with the lender's approval, should include a mortgagee's clause, and should contain all pertinent information to determine that the required coverage is included.

An investor may waive an escrow account in total or for specific escrow items, such as hazard insurance, even though the documentation provides for their collection. Many times in granting a waiver, it will be conditioned so that should the mortgagor fail to pay the items or the loan goes into default for another reason, the escrow account may be reactivated. Extreme caution should be taken in waiving escrow deposits. Even though the loan documents may require escrow deposits, once they have been waived, it can be very difficult to get the mortgagor to begin making deposits, even if an event of default has taken place.

■ Types of Insurance Coverage

Generally, investors will require one or more of the following types of insurance on income properties:

Fire, Extended Coverage, and Vandalism

This coverage insures against direct loss to property caused by fire, smoke, lightning, windstorm, hail, aircraft, vehicles, explosion, riot, civil commotion, vandalism, and malicious mischief.

All Risk Coverage

Coverage under this type of policy insures against all risks of direct physical loss, subject to specified exclusions. It is important to review the major exclusions in each policy, which generally include floods, earthquakes, and back-up of sewers and drains. While this coverage is usually preferable to the named perils policy described above, there is no true "all risk" coverage.

Builders Risk Insurance

Buildings in the course of construction are covered under this type of policy, which may be written on either a named perils or all risk basis. This property is usually insured for its completed value. Unless specifically endorsed, builders risk policies do not usually allow for occupancy. Therefore, when construction is complete, a permanent policy should be written.

Rent Insurance

This coverage indemnifies for loss of income from a rental property as a result of fire or other insured perils.

Business Income Coverage

An all-purpose Business Income form insures business operations for loss of income brought about by a necessary suspension of operations arising from fire or other insured perils. The form includes Rental Value insurance and Extra Expense coverage.

Boiler and Machinery Insurance

This coverage pays for the loss from damage by a sudden and accidental break-down of boiler equipment, refrigeration and air conditioning equipment, electrical apparatus, and a wide variety of other machinery.

Flood Insurance

Federal regulations require flood insurance for properties located in special flood hazard areas if the mortgage is obtained from a federally insured or regulated lender. When a property is located in Flood Zone A, flood insurance should be provided. If the finished floor elevation is three feet above the 100-year flood plain, flood insurance can be waived.

The National Flood Insurance Program is federally subsidized. Maximum amounts of coverage from $100,000 to $300,000 are available depending on the program being used in the community where the property is located and the construction of the property. Flood coverage should also be required for any area that might be affected by a hurricane.

General Liability Insurance

This coverage pays on behalf of the insured all sums which the insured becomes legally obligated to pay as damages because of bodily injury or property damage.

Umbrella Liability Insurance

This policy provides an amount of excess liability coverage and protects the insured from exclusions and gaps in the primary liability policy that serves as the underlying insurance.

Miscellaneous Coverage

There are special types of coverage for different operations that may apply to the mortgaged property, such as product liability, liquor liability, or crime coverage.

Self-Insurance

Some large companies set aside sufficient reserves to provide their own insurance protection. However, self-insurance should not be accepted from any company without the investor's approval.

■ Insurance Policy Considerations

Carrier Eligibility

When an insurance policy is received, the first step in making sure it is acceptable is to determine whether the carrier meets the investor's requirements. These requirements will typically include some or all of the following:

- The carrier must be licensed to transact business in the state in which the property is located.
- The carrier must have been in business at least five years.
- The carrier must carry a policyholder's rating of A or better in the most recent issue of Best's Key Rating Guide and a financial size category rating of Class IV or better, which would give it a policyholder surplus of at least $5 million.

■ Some investors may require that in any one risk, the face amount of coverage acceptable from one carrier should not exceed a certain percentage of the carrier's paid-in capital and surplus unless the loan administrator is furnished with reinsurance endorsements or letters from reinsuring carriers meeting the same paid-in capital and surplus requirements on their share of the total coverage.

It is of utmost importance that particular attention is paid to the strength and solvency of the insurance carrier covering the mortgaged property.

Insurance Policy Acceptability

After the loan administrator determines that the carrier meets the investor's requirements, it should turn its attention to the policy. The mortgagee usually requires that the property be insured for its full replacement value. In some instances, consent may be given to reduce the hazard insurance coverage from full replacement value to the actual cash value.

Sometimes the investor may allow the policy to be written for the outstanding principal balance, provided there is no coinsurance and, in the loan administrator's opinion, the investor will be adequately protected. In cases where consent is given to a reduction in insurance coverage, it is expected that the mortgagor will be advised that he or she is self-insured for the amount of equity in the property.

■ Insurance Clauses and Endorsements

Deductible Clause

Most policies contain deductible clauses applicable to the property coverage, and they should be acceptable to the investor provided the amount of the deductible is reasonable in relation to the coverage written. For example, a $1 million policy might reasonably contain a $5,000 deductible clause.

Special Endorsements and Mortgage Clauses

There are a number of special endorsements and clauses the loan administrator should look for in every policy. The attachment of a standard mortgage clause to every policy is the most important requirement because it protects the mortgagee's interest and provides the following:

■ Thirty days advance notice must be given in writing if the policy is cancelled for any reason.

■ Investors must be named in the mortgage clause, which must include their full corporate name and require that any loss be paid to investors as mortgagees. This clause must be written into the policy on a noncontribution form, which provides that in the event of loss, the interest of the mortgagee is not impaired by any act of neglect of the mortgagor, any foreclosure or notice of sale, any change in title or ownership of the property or by any occupation of the premises for purposes more hazardous than those permitted by the policy. In all instances where the investor's interests are shown on either the policy or the endorsements, the full name and address should be used. The investor may be named as loss payee under loss of rents coverage as well as building coverage.

■ Each policy must contain a waiver of subrogation clause or endorsement. This provision is currently incorporated in most property policies. Under the term of the policy issued, the insuring company may require that the insured assigns to it any and all rights of recovery in case of an insured loss, as against any other party who is responsible for the fire loss. To protect the interests of the mortgagee and also those of the tenants occupying the premises, all policies submitted should contain this waiver of subrogation clause. The context of the particular clause varies at times because of the wording of a policy issued by the particular company or because of policies issued within certain states. In general, the loan administrator should accept policies bearing clauses that are written similar to the following: "It is hereby stipulated that this insurance (coverage) shall not be invalidated should the insured waive in writing, prior to any loss, all rights of recovery against any party (or investor and tenant names) for a loss occurring to the property described herein."

■ Vacancy and/or unoccupancy endorsements should be obtained when necessary. Should a vacancy be discovered by the loan administrator, it should be reported immediately to the carrier and the mortgagor should be billed for any premium increase.

Coinsurance

The true purpose of the coinsurance clause is to distribute the cost of insurance equitably among property owners. Insurance companies have universally adopted the clause, and its fairness is demonstrated by the companies' willingness to reduce the rate or cost of insurance for the acceptance of this clause. The operation of the clause furnishes an incentive to the owner to insure his or her property fully and to increase insurance when there is an appreciation in values.

The coinsurance clause is not as complicated as it might seem. In fact, it is rather simple when thoroughly understood. In brief, the clause is an agreement between the insured and the company. It requires that the insured parties maintain insurance on their properties equal to a certain percentage of their value. When insured parties carry sufficient insurance to comply with the coinsurance clause, they will be entitled to collect the entire actual loss, not to exceed the amount of the policy.

If the parties fail to carry sufficient insurance, then in the event of loss, they must bear their share of the loss just as though they were an insurance company. In other words, the insured may collect only that proportion of the loss which the amount of insurance carried bears to the amount of insurance the insured should have carried under the terms of the coinsurance clause. The examples below illustrate this concept.

> **Amount of Insurance Carried × Amount of Loss =**
> **Amount Collectible ÷ Amount of Insurance Required**

Obviously, the key to coinsurance is accurate computation of the building's value. By using the services available from firms such as Marshall and Swift Publication Company in Los Angeles, California, the loan administrator can compute the building's value as long as the loan administrator has access to a dated appraisal and information on construction type and property location.

Example No. 1   Insured Carried Sufficient Insurance

Actual cash value of property	$100,000
Amount of insurance required to be carried	
by the 80% coinsurance clause	
(80% of $100,000)	$ 80,000
Loss sustained	$ 40,000
Amount collectible from insurance company	$ 40,000

In Example 1 above, the insured collects his or her loss in full.

Example No. 2   Insured Did Not Carry Sufficient Insurance

Actual cash value of property	$100,000
Amount of insurance required to be carried	
by the 80% coinsurance clause	
(80% of $100,000)	$ 80,000
Insurance actually carried	$ 60,000
Loss sustained	$ 40,000
Amount collectible from insurance company	$ 30,000

In Example 2 above, the insured must contribute $10,000.

Agreed Amount Clause

This clause is basically an endorsement by the insuring company that the amount of insurance written satisfies the coinsurance requirement. It serves as a waiver of any coinsurance penalties and should be added to policies whenever possible. Endorsements usually must be renewed or extended every year, so the loan administrator should follow up at the end of each such period.

Replacement Cost Endorsement

Under this endorsement the insurance on buildings covers the actual cost of repairs or replacement without deduction for depreciation. It is important to remember that if this endorsement is attached to the policy, then the coinsurance clause applies to replacement cost and not actual cash value. A claim adjusted to actual cash value may be insufficient to restore the property and thus have a damaging effect on the property's cash flow. Some companies require that a Statement of Values be filed each year to keep this endorsement on the policy.

■ Renewal and Replacement Insurance

Even when the investor holds the original policy, securing and reviewing renewal policies is usually the loan administrator's responsibility. If renewal coverage is not received by the loan administrator at least ten days before expiration (or a date determined by the investor's policy or loan documents), the borrower should be notified immediately to provide renewal coverage.

Notification should include a statement that the investor will place coverage at the borrower's expense in the event of noncompliance. The notification should be confirmed in writing by certified mail with a return receipt and a copy of the letter sent to the investor. If acceptable renewal insurance is not received by the day prior to expiration, the loan administrator should notify the investor and the mortgagor by telephone and then (with the investor's approval) secure the required coverage at the mortgagor's expense.

If any required policy or coverage on a mortgage being serviced is cancelled for any reason and the mortgagor has not furnished acceptable replacement insurance, the loan administrator (with the investor's approval) should order the appropriate insurance coverage at the mortgagor's expense. To calculate the required coverage for renewals or replacement, the loan administrator should calculate property valuation to ensure that the amount and types of coverage carried bear a reasonable relationship to the value of the security and the risks to which the property is exposed. For this purpose, the loan administrator may again use the Marshall and Swift Publication Company's Valuation Service.

When replacement or renewal policies are received, they should be originals. In many states copies of insurance policies are unacceptable and in violation of insurance laws regarding first mortgages. When the loan administrator retains the original policy, the investor may require the loan administrator to provide an insurance certification or summary. Figure 4.1 provides a sample of an insurance checklist. It should also be noted that original policies should never be released or returned for cancellation or substitution until an acceptable substitute policy has been received, reviewed, and found acceptable.

When a mortgage is paid in full, it is usually the loan administrator's responsibility to see that the policy is returned to the mortgagor and to take the necessary steps to eliminate the mortgagee's interest from the policy. When the mortgage is paid in full through an escrow agent, it is acceptable to forward the policy to that agent.

Blanket Insurance

Frequently, owners of income properties will include several properties under blanket insurance coverage. The loan administrator must be sure that the mortgaged property covered under the blanket policy is adequately insured. If the original master policy cannot be obtained, a copy of the original policy certified as a true copy of the original should be secured. Occasionally these policies are so voluminous that it is acceptable to obtain an underlying endorsement specifying the mortgaged location and that no less than the proper amount of coverage applies to this location. All pertinent forms, along with a mortgage clause, should be attached to the endorsement with a statement that at least ten days prior notice shall be given the mortgagee if there are any reductions or cancellations of coverage. Certificates should not be considered acceptable evidence of property coverage since the insuring company confers no rights on the certificate holder and the actual extent of coverage is often hard to determine.

Force Placed Coverage

A number of insurance companies issue a policy designed to protect both the mortgagee and mortgagor on income properties when no evidence of renewal coverage is offered. Typically, these policies offer a limited amount of insurance ($500,000 or $1 million) on an automatic basis along with an option to purchase additional coverage on individual risks. When a loan administrator has purchased this type of policy, the premium should be billed to the borrower if coverage was renewed in this manner on mortgaged property.

Figure 4.1 | Sample Insurance Checklist

LOAN # _____ DATE:_____

Investor: _____ Investor #: _____

Borrower Name: _____

Property Name: _____ _____

Property Location: _____

_____

Insurance Company: _____

Address: _____

Company Rating: _____ Per _____ Best's Key Rating Guide _____

5% of Policyholder's surplus is_____

Policy #: _____

Policy Dates: _____

Premium: _____Loan Administrator Pays _____ Borrower Pays_____

	Coverage	Coinsurance

BUILDINGS $ _____   _____

CONTENTS _____   _____

LOSS OF RENTS_____   _____

LIABILITY_____   _____

OTHER _____   _____

BLANKET BASIS   Yes ( )   No ( )   N/A ( )

ENDORSEMENTS ATTACHED:

Correct Mortgagee Clause   Yes ( )   No ( )   Date Requested_____

Loss Payable Clause   Yes ( )   No ( )   Date Requested_____

Special 30-Day Cancellation   Yes ( )   No ( )   Date Requested_____

Waiver of Subrogation   Yes ( )   No ( )   Date Requested_____

Replacement Cost   Yes ( )   No ( )   Date Requested_____

Agreed Amount Endorsement   Yes ( )   No ( )   Date Requested_____

Sch. of Values (Master Pol)   Yes ( )   No ( )   Date Requested_____

Inflation Clause   Yes ( )   No ( )   Date Requested_____

Paid Receipt   Yes ( )   No ( )   Date Requested_____

Other _____

AGENCY:_____

ADDRESS:_____

PHONE NUMBER:_____

OTHER COMMENTS:_____

■ Insurance Loss Settlements

General Procedures

Monitoring insurance losses is a critical function of every servicer and lender to ensure that the collateral is restored to its original condition. Care must be taken to insure that all repairs are completed properly and that the contractors or any other vendors do not file any liens against the property.

In the event of a loss, the intention of the mortgagor regarding the restoration of the property should be determined immediately. Loan documents frequently give the investor an option of either applying the insurance proceeds to the loan balance or using them for restoring the property. Therefore, the loan documents should be checked to ascertain the options available and provisions agreed to previously.

Investors will establish their own limits and guidelines for a loan administrator's responsibilities. For example, if the limit is based upon an agreed amount or percentage of value, the loan administrator will usually not be required to inspect repairs for a loss of less than that amount. In this situation, the loan administrator should obtain a copy of the proof of loss and an affidavit from the mortgagor that the damage has been repaired and the property restored to its original condition. Additionally, the loan administrator will be required to obtain waivers of lien from all involved contractors, including subcontractors. (See Figures 4.2 and 4.3 for samples of contractor statements and owner certification.) When these two tasks have been accomplished, the hazard insurance loss draft can be endorsed and disbursed. In the event of a delinquency or foreclosure the loan administrator may want to apply the proceeds to the outstanding principal balance.

In preparing to endorse or disburse a loss draft, the loan administrator must determine that the total loss is represented by the draft. If coverage is distributed among carriers, the total of all drafts should not exceed the agreed upon limit. For losses over the limit, the loan administrator should immediately inspect the premises to determine the extent of damage and require the mortgagor to take the necessary steps to secure the protection of the remaining improvements. The investor should then be contacted and supplied with a statement of intention from the mortgagor, an inspection report and photographs, and the loan administrator's recommendation for applying the insurance proceeds.

If the loan administrator's recommendation to make the loss drafts available for restoration is approved, the borrower should be informed immediately. If the loss is less than the agreed upon limit, the investor may authorize the loan administrator to hold the drafts until receipted bills and lien waivers are submitted. Or the loan administrator may be authorized to place the monies in a non-interest-bearing escrow account pending future disbursement upon restoration.

Under certain circumstances the loan administrator may make partial distributions from the escrow account during restoration. If the loss is greater than the agreed upon limit, the investor will likely handle the disbursement directly. When this happens, the loan administrator must forward the names of contractors and others with the amounts due for repairs.

Figure 4.2 | Sample Contractor Statement

(INVESTOR)

(CC/O LOAN ADMINISTRATOR)

(ADDRESS)

GENTLEMEN:

Re: _____ (Kind of Damage)

_____ (Name of Mortgagor)

_____ (Property Address)

Cost of Repairs $ _____

In connection with the captioned claim, all necessary repairs have been completed and the following statements are hereby submitted as required by your regulations:

STATEMENT OF CONTRACTOR

I certify that I have furnished all labor and materials for repairs necessitated because of _____ damage occurring on the _____ day of _____ to the property located at _____. The repairs have been completed in a professional manner at a total cost of $ _____, and a bill for a like amount has been rendered to _____.

I further certify that the amount of this bill has been paid to me, or satisfactory arrangements have been made for payment from proceeds of the loss draft when received by the assured mortgagor, and that no liens against said property exist as a result of the above repairs or will exist after payment to me of the $_____ specified as total cost of same.

_____

Contractor (Signature)

Figure 4.3 | Sample Owner Certification

(INVESTOR)
(CC/O LOAN ADMINISTRATOR)
(ADDRESS)

OWNER'S CERTIFICATION

GENTLEMEN:

Re: _____ (Kind of Damage)

_____ (Name of Mortgagor)

_____ (Property Address)

Amount of Loss Drafts $ _____

Date of Loss   _____

In connection with the captioned claim, all necessary repairs have been completed and the following statement is hereby submitted as required by your regulations.

Referring to the loss incurred by the above-referenced property, this is to certify that the property has been restored to the same condition as before the loss and that no liens will remain outstanding in connection with repairs and restoration of this property.

Sincerely,

_____

(Mortgagor)

_____

(Date)

The loan administrator should inspect the property again after restoration to make sure the work has been completed in a satisfactory manner. The loan administrator should forward all bills for work and materials to ensure that no mechanic's or material liens will be placed against the property after disbursement of the previously reported amount.

If the mortgagee decides to apply the monies against the outstanding loan balance, rather than to restoration, the transaction should be handled as a large prepayment or prepayment in full. If this results in a prepayment in full, prepayment penalties will not usually be charged to the borrower.

The following checklists outline some of the common loss draft procedures:

Notifications

- Advise the borrower immediately upon report of any loss. If possible, provide details of damage and complete the inspection as soon as possible.
- Notify the insurance carrier of the lender's interest in the policy and specify that all loss drafts must include the lender as payee.
- Request that a copy of the adjuster's report be provided as soon as possible to report details to the lender and to be used to monitor the repairs.
- Obtain copies of all contracts and receipts to monitor disbursements.
- Review specific procedures of the lender to ensure compliance with all requirements. Special attention must be paid to unique forms and procedures for check endorsement.

Monitor Repairs and Disbursements

Prior to each disbursement, the servicer should submit documentation to the lender and request approval to release the draw request. This documentation may include the following:

- Inspection reports
- Lien waivers
- Photographs
- Progress Report of Repairs

The servicer should verify with each lender as well as consult the mortgage document for each loan for any additional items that may be required.

Special Handling Considerations

The loss may be so significant that it may require additional handling, such as the following:

- Interest bearing accounts.
- Consultants to monitor reconstruction.
- Forbearance if loss of rents coverage is exhausted.
- If insurance loss proceeds exceed the loan balance, the lender may require the debt to be paid in full.
- Special handling for loans in foreclosure or workout.
- The lender may instruct the servicer to withhold retainage.

■ Environmental Insurance Issues

Lenders face serious financial exposure from the threat of environmentally impaired property with the possible imposition of liability existing under federal and state statutes. Given the potential sources for the imposition of environmental liability, the Environmental Protection Agency (EPA) has attempted to provide a safety net under the Comprehensive Environmental Response Compensation and Liability Act (CERCLA) and the Resource Conservation and Recovery Act (RCRA) by promulgating the *Final Rule.* This rule attempts to state the circumstances under which lenders would not be deemed "participating in the management" or "influencing" the control, handling, or disposal of hazardous materials at a borrower's property and, therefore, would not be liable for their remediation.

However, there are several significant reasons why the *Final Rule* cannot or may not provide immunity to a lender, including the following:

- ■ The *Final Rule* does not apply to state or common law.
- ■ The *Final Rule* is subject to ongoing legal challenges.

Within the *Final Rule* the EPA reserves the right to seek "equitable reimbursement" if the EPA believes a property holder has been unjustly enriched as a result of an EPA cleanup. Most importantly, while the *Final Rule* may be able to absolve a lender of federal liability for environmental liability, it cannot assure that a borrower can continue monthly payments and that the collateral remains unimpaired.

■ Environmental Risks

Program Guidelines for Lenders

A comprehensive environmental risk program should assure that the lender avoids, or at least limits, its liability for environmental impairment and also that the borrower remains able to fulfill its loan obligations. If not, the loan collateral should be free from environmental impairment. Several insurance companies are providing policies that achieve this goal by incorporating the following features:

- ■ The borrower is the primary insured (and is responsible for the premium); the lender is mortgagee or additional named insured; and the policy is assignable to a purchaser.
- ■ The policy affords coverage for the following:
  - ■ Liability for environmental cleanup
  - ■ Expenses pertaining to claim and legal defense
  - ■ Cleanup and remediation costs
- ■ The policy responds to environmental impairment claims that either preexisted the policy and were undiscovered by a preacquisition assessment (Phase I audit) or are discovered or occur subsequent to the inception of the policy.
- ■ The policy covers contamination which results from operations of tenants as well as contamination caused by third parties.

Advantages of Program

■ The adequacy of the Phase I is insured because a policy was issued. The insurance company is responsible for the due diligence. This responsibility is removed from the asset manager.

■ The borrower may be protected from default through coverage of cleanup costs and has an incentive to remediate the contamination.

■ Legal costs are covered whether or not the lender is responsible for cleanup costs.

■ Coverage speeds consummation of deals or enables the closing of some which might not otherwise happen.

■ Assignability of the policy can add value to the property by eliminating any concern of unknown contamination for a purchaser.

■ Financing a property should be quicker and easier.

■ In some instances, personal environmental indemnification can be waived.

Limits of Coverage and Cost

Typical coverage for a borrower is $2,000,000 per contamination, with $2,000,000 aggregate and a deductible of $10,000. A three-year policy premium is approximately $9,000 to $12,000. Unusual circumstances may increase premiums. For properties with larger exposures, increased limits of coverage are available with corresponding premium increases.

Portfolio Coverage

An insurance coverage program where the borrower obtains coverage at loan inception, or, for existing loans, at the time of renewal or modification, will leave a portion of a lender's present portfolio without the benefit of insurance coverage. This can be addressed by procuring "portfolio coverage" which offers the same basic policy coverage but to the lender only. There are several types of portfolio coverage on the market.

The creation and implementation of an environmental risk reduction program is a response to the management of significant risks facing both the lender and the borrower. The insurance coverage, if viewed from the perspective of the lender, is another tool in the management of credit risks like fire, casualty, or title insurance.

When viewed from the perspective of the borrower, the insurance requirement offers protection that is increasingly procured by the borrower or principals of the borrower as individual protection from liability associated with personal environmental indemnifications. The property as collateral is protected from impairment by the coverage afforded if either preexisting contamination or subsequent contamination is discovered. The property, as an asset of the borrower, is enhanced in value by the insurance and its assignability.

The environmental status of a mortgaged property must be discovered prior to the funding of a mortgage loan. This environmental assessment must be a part of the loan underwriting with the asset managers assuming responsibility for the evaluation of the property.

New Loans

A Phase I audit, also known as a preacquisition site assessment, must be ordered on all new loans. A Phase I audit can detect most contamination and substantially reduce the risk. The asset manager must perform a due diligence for evaluating the potential environmental risk.

Loan Renewals, E&F Rated Loans

When a loan is renewed or downgraded to an E or F quality rating, the asset manager must determine the exposure to the risk of liability and evaluate the following:

- Has the property changed since loan inception?
- Have the tenants changed (e.g., any paint stores, dry cleaners, photo labs)?
- Is there any environmental risk associated with the borrower (e.g., industrial operation)?
- Are there any changes in the surrounding area?

A Phase I audit should be ordered and a due diligence performed using the same guidelines as for a new loan. The responsibility for monitoring compliance with the environmental due diligence lies with the asset manager. The Environmental Coverage Requirement pertains to all loans secured by commercial real estate. The borrower must provide, prior to loan closing, environmental liability insurance as follows:

Policy Statement

- Names the borrower as insured and the lender as additional named insured.
- Covers the property location.
- Has a maximum deductible of $10,000.
- Contains policy limits of at least $2,000,000 per discovery and $2,000,000 in aggregate for cleanup costs.
- Cannot be cancelled for at least three years and is automatically renewed by annual premium payment.

Policy Requirements

Provided coverage should include the following:

- Legal liability.
- Expenses associated with claim defense.
- Legal defense expenses.
- "Clean-up" or remediation expenses that are imposed by legal statutes, or from common law remedies, due to contamination that was present on the property but unknown prior to the policy inception.
  a) "Discovery" of contamination during the policy period.
  b) Responds immediately to claims where the borrower is subject to legal liability pursuant to statute, or other common law remedy.
  c) Responds to a claim which is a written demand by a third party or governmental agency.

d) Names lender as an additional named insured entitled to full coverage under the policy, for covered claims and where the lender is subject to potential position of legal liability pursuant to statute.

e) Extends coverage to borrower and lender for third-party contamination that occurs after that policy is issued.

f) Responds to claims for contamination to the insured's property for which the insured may be liable pursuant to statute or common law remedy.

g) Provides for loans over $1,000,000, that coverage is provided to lender for contamination accidentally caused by a tenant which occurs after the policy inception, whereby the lender is potentially legally obligated pursuant to statute or common law to a third party and coverage is afforded to the lender without a foreclosure upon the property.

■ Tax and Assessment Procedures

Real Estate Tax and Municipal Assessments

All income-producing real estate is subject to real estate tax and other municipal assessments, unless exempted or abated (i.e., a church). The real estate tax assessments are usually a percentage of the market value and are imposed at the local level by the state, a school district, county, township, borough, or city. Taxes and/or assessments are billed quarterly, semiannually, or annually. In establishing tax records, the servicer should review all property legal descriptions to ensure that all tax parcel descriptions will be obtained. Because real estate taxes are assessed against and records are maintained in numbered tax parcels, the loan administrator must be careful to coordinate each tax parcel against the legal description of the mortgaged property to assure that it covers the same real estate tract.

Income property mortgage documentation provides that real estate taxes and lienable assessments be paid before penalties accrue and usually requires evidence of payment. It also states that if taxes and assessments are not paid, the nonpayment creates a default in the mortgage.

Many times the documents give the investor the option either to permit the mortgagor to pay the assessments directly or require that an escrow be established to be used for payment as bills are issued. There was once a universal trend to require tax escrows, which assure both servicer and investor that bills will be secured and paid, rather than leaving payment to the discretion of the mortgagor. In many deals in the 1980s, the escrow deposits were waived by a side-letter agreement as long as no defaults existed. In the 1990s this trend was reversed because of the many problems with real estate loans in the 1990s.

Procedures

The loan administrator needs to establish correct procedures to ensure that real estate taxes and other property assessments are paid promptly. If an escrow account is required, the loan administrator should use the procedures discussed in the following section on escrow analysis, keeping in mind that it is important that all assessments be paid.

When bills are issued, the loan administrator should review them to make sure they have the correct property description, title holder, assessment, and amount.

The bills should be paid promptly to avoid penalties. If the mortgagor is required to pay taxes and assessments directly, the loan administrator must make sure the mortgagor has done so in order to certify to the investor that the assessments have been paid. To do this, the loan administrator can require the mortgagor to present receipted bills for inspection, conduct its own tax search, or use the services of a tax service bureau to determine payment. Whether the loan administrator decides to make a search or has a tax bureau perform the task, it is important the records be checked carefully to ensure that all taxes have been paid.

Handling Unpaid Taxes and Assessments

Real estate taxes on income property involve sizable sums of money, and, if they and other assessments are not paid, the property may be subject to liens and possible sale. If the loan administrator learns that taxes have not been paid, appropriate measures should be taken to determine the reason and require that the assessments be paid within a fixed period of time.

If arrangements cannot be made or are not kept, the loan administrator must be prepared to recommend action to the investor to protect its interests. This is critical inasmuch as tax liens are superior to any mortgage lien, and if a property goes to tax sale, it is conceivable that the investor's mortgage lien may be wiped out. If legal proceedings are started, it may be necessary for the investor to advance the funds in order to prevent the property from going to a tax sale. Property tax advances are customarily permitted to be added to the mortgage loan balance. It may also be necessary to wait until the foreclosure sale, at which time all outstanding tax and municipal assessments will have to be paid. Penalties should be considered when making a recommendation because the investor will be responsible for paying them.

■ Summary

This Chapter covered the escrow procedures used by loan administrators, the types of mortgage insurance policies, common insurance loss settlement procedures, and the taxes and assessments common to commercial real estate. The loan administrator is responsible for the administration of a borrower's escrow account. The administrator insures the timely payment of taxes, assessments, and insurance, and rectifies situations involving a surplus or deficit of escrow funds.

To protect their interest in real estate, investors require many types of insurance coverage on income properties. The policies cover things such as fire, vandalism, rent, flood damage, personal and property liability, and builder risks.

When acquiring insurance, the lender must insure the carrier is eligible to provide the needed coverage and that the policies meet investor requirements. Important clauses and endorsements included in most policies include the deductible clause, agreed amount clause, replacement cost endorsement, and any applicable special endorsements.

Monitoring insurance losses is critical to insure that collateral is restored to its original condition. Lenders and servicers must be sure that investor requirements are adhered to and effectively executed. Loan documents usually provide investors with the option of applying proceeds to the loan balance or using the funds to restore the property.

Under federal and state statutes, lenders face serious financial repercussions resulting from environmentally impaired property. Because of this, it is imperative that lenders carry comprehensive environmental coverage to avoid or limit environmentally related losses.

Finally, all income-producing real estate is subject to taxes and municipal assessments. The loan administrator must insure that taxes and assessments are current to protect the interests of concerned parties.

■ Chapter 4 Review Questions

1. When should a mortgage escrow account be analyzed?

   a. Semi-annually

   b. During refinancing

   c. Every time funds are disbursed

2. Who determines the amount of monthly escrow to be paid by a mortgagor?

   a. Investor

   b. Escrow agent

   c. Loan processor

   d. Loan administrator

3. Check four types of insurance available for income properties.

   ____ Rent insurance

   ____ Business asset coverage

   ____ Umbrella liability

   ____ Boiler and machinery

   ____ Builders construction

   ____ Fire, extended coverage, and vandalism

4. Flood insurance can be waived if the finished floor elevation is how many feet above the 100-year flood plain?

   a. 3 feet

   b. 5 feet

   c. 10 feet

   d. 15 feet

5. Which is *NOT* a common endorsement or clause found in mortgage-related insurance policies?

   a. Coinsurance clause

   b. Agreed amount clause

   c. Special endorsements

   d. Replacement cost endorsement

   e. Market value replacement clause

6. Which clause is an agreement between the insured and the company stating the insured will maintain property insurance equal to a certain percentage of its value?

   a. Coinsurance

   b. Market value

   c. Agreed amount

   d. Replacement cost

7. Which term describes an insurance payment that settles a claim for damages to mortgaged property?

   a. Loss draft

   b. Reimbursement

   c. Value replacement

   d. Mitigating settlement

8. Which is not a special consideration when handling significant property loss?

   a. Use of consultants to monitor reconstruction

   b. Special handling of loans in workout or foreclosure

   c. Forbearance if loss of rents coverage is exhausted

   d. Refinancing if loss proceeds exceed the loan balance

9. A Phase 1 audit, which is designed to detect contamination, is also called a(n)

   a. environmental site review.

   b. pre-closing property review.

   c. preacquisition site assessment.

   d. due diligence preliminary assessment.

10. When determining needs for an environmental insurance policy, lenders should include all of the following *EXCEPT*

    a. lender is named primary insured.

    b. expenses for legal defense cleanup.

    c. pre-existing environmental impairment claims.

    d. contamination claims caused by tenants and third-parties.

11. Tax liens are superior to any mortgage liens.

    a. True

    b. False

12. Tax assessments on income-producing property are usually a percentage of the

    a. market value.

    b. appraised value.

    c. principal balance.

    d. sum of annual principal and interest.

Financial Statements and Lease Analysis

learning objectives

Upon completion of this chapter, you should be able to

■ identify the basic financial factors used in the analysis of property performance;

■ distinguish the elements of a lease to be evaluated by a loan servicer;

■ recognize the special provisions in shopping center leases;

■ identify the clauses in a lease relating to legal issues; and

■ determine the credit instruments that are monitored in commercial real estate servicing.

■ Introduction

Financial statements provide a good understanding of how well the security property is performing and the overall financial condition of the mortgagor. Investors recognize the benefits of an annual review of the statements; therefore, most loan documents require the mortgagor to submit certified financial statements for the property and/or borrowing entity after the close of the fiscal or calendar year.

Financial statements of the tenant and guarantor of the loan may also be required. Depending on the investor and property type, the loan documents may require quarterly financial statements. The loan documents govern the required format and content of the statements and will usually state whether or not the statements are to be audited, compiled by a CPA, or certified by the mortgagor.

The mortgagor should be notified of the financial statement requirements at closing and at least 90 days prior to the due date of the statements to encourage timely receipt of the statements. Failure by the mortgagor to submit annual statements is generally considered a default under the loan documents and may warrant further action. If statements are unobtainable, gather information from other sources such as recent property inspections and rent rolls to determine the significance. Depending on the significance and the loan documents, other options may be pursued, such as an audit of the borrower's books or a demand letter. It is important to have a system in place to record receipt of the statements. Send written reminders if the statements are not received by the due date. Keep copies of annual statements and the analysis in chronological order to provide historical information for future reference.

■ Financial Statement Analysis

It is important to analyze the financial statements to determine whether or not the property is performing in accordance with pro forma statements. Items inconsistent within the pro forma statements should be questioned. It is helpful to use a form for analyzing financial statements. Some investors may require their own forms be completed by the loan administrator and/or mortgagor. Compare income, expenses, and net operating income with original projections and prior years. If possible, statements should be reviewed in conjunction with the annual inspection to obtain an overall understanding of the performance of security property.

The person analyzing the financial statements should have a financial background with knowledge of generally accepted accounting principles. It should be determined whether statements are prepared on a cash or accrual basis of accounting, as it will affect computation of net operating income. If the statements are audited by a CPA, note whether or not an "unqualified" opinion is given. Also, if the statements are audited by a CPA, review the footnote section, as it can be a source of important information such as transfers in ownership, placement of subordinate debt, pending litigation, unrecorded receivables, insurance claims, etc. If the auditor's opinion is "qualified," review the exceptions.

Statements compiled or reviewed only by a CPA (i.e., no opinion is provided) or statements prepared internally by the mortgagor should at least be certified to be true and correct by the mortgagor. It is important to remember that the loan documents govern the required format and any deviation requires approval by the investor.

The basic financial statement information to be analyzed is as follows:

Income

- Compare annual income to a current, certified rent roll, noting any trends or unusual variances. It is important to note any leases expiring within the next 12 months and the effect to income.

- Note additional income generators such as interest income, vending machines, late charges, security deposits, insurance proceeds, etc.

- Determine if all tenants have paid expense reimbursements in accordance with their lease agreements. It is helpful to have the mortgagor include the annual tenant reimbursement amounts on the rent roll.

Expenses

- Compare actual operating expenses to market expenses and investigate major variances. For example, management fees typically range from 3 percent to 6 percent of gross income depending on the property type. Fees that exceed the high range should be investigated.

■ Identify any capital expenditures or nonrecurring expenses such as roof replacement or new construction.

■ Compare expense items such as utilities, taxes, and insurance to the prior year to determine any trends. Investigate substantial increases or decreases.

■ Identify any payments to subordinate lien holders.

■ Pay particular attention to any unusual expense items or cash contributions to partners, as this may indicate funds are being diverted from the property.

■ Determine if a full year's insurance and tax expense are included in the expenses by confirming tax and insurance amounts from paid receipts on file.

Computation of Net Operating Income and Debt Coverage Ratio

■ The debt coverage ratio is computed by dividing annual net operating income before debt service by annual debt service. Debt service includes principal and interest payments to the investor. Calculate debt coverage ratios for first lien debt and subordinate debt separately.

■ Exclude all noncash expenses such as depreciation and amortization when computing net operating income before debt service.

■ Exclude cash contributions from the mortgagor, capital improvements, etc., when computing net operating income.

■ Net operating income should be sufficient to cover annual debt service payments for first lien and subordinate lien debt. Special attention should be given to debt coverage ratios below 1.15.

All questionable items or unusual variances should be discussed with the mortgagor. The loan administrator should forward the statements to the investor along with its analysis. Additionally, comments regarding the statements or explanations of unusual items as discussed with the mortgagor should be furnished to the investor.

When reviewing the annual statements, pay attention to any special loan document provisions such as participations, debt service holdbacks, repair holdbacks, etc., because additional steps may need to be taken. Subordinate debt and wrap notes may also have special review requirements. It is the loan administrator's responsibility to make sure there is compliance with any special provisions.

Problem Statements

If the loan administrator's analysis indicates negative net operating income, a reduction in the debt coverage ratio from the prior year, or unusual variances, further research may be necessary. This may include a discussion with the mortgagor and an inspection of the property to determine the extent of the problem. The loan administrator may enlist the expertise of the firm's production department or consult local leasing brokers or market publications for further insight into rental rates and market vacancies. It is the loan administrator's role to determine the nature of the problem and what effect it will have on the viability of the loan. Loan administrators should always notify the investor of their findings and monitor the loan until the problem is resolved.

◼ Lease Analysis

The lease is a contract that creates and defines the legal relationship between the landlord or lessor and the tenant or lessee. In exchange for payment of rent and other considerations, the landlord (the owner of the real estate) grants to the tenant the right to possession and use of all or part of the property, subject to certain terms and conditions, for a specified period of time. In most types of commercial real estate (the major exception being hotels and motels) lease income provides the bulk of revenues available to service the mortgage loan; thus, understanding and accurate evaluation of lease terms and conditions is crucial to underwriting a loan. Lease obligations often require post-closing management by loan administrators as well.

There are two primary considerations in lease analysis from the investor's perspective:

1. Poorly drafted leases can create economic problems for the borrower that may jeopardize his or her ability to make loan payments.
2. If the investor takes the property back, he or she will have to live with the terms and conditions of the lease, unless provision is made that the investor has the option to terminate it. In most foreclosure situations, however, tenants paying rent are a valuable commodity.

The lease should be evaluated in accordance with the items below:

The Parties

The parties to the lease must be accurately defined, including the correctly spelled full name of each party, the nature of the legal form (usually individual, partnership, or corporation), and the state of domicile for the partnership, or corporation. Individuals may sign for themselves, any general partner for a partnership, and the president or secretary for a corporation. If there is any question on a corporation, a copy of the resolution of the Board of Directors granting signing authority should be attached. If the signer is acting as an agent for a principal, written authority from that principal should be attached.

Demised Premises

Demised premises should be precisely identified, in terms of building address, floor number, suite/store number, and area in square feet to be leased. A floor plan or drawing of the space in relation to the entire property is very helpful. Inadequate identification can invalidate the lease. The lease should also state whether parking rights are exclusive or nonexclusive, whether specific parking spaces are designated for the tenant and, if so, the number and locations of such spaces. Separate charges for parking should be noted by the reviewer.

Term

The term of the lease should be stipulated, in years and odd months. Lease commencement and termination dates should be clearly stated, as well as the date the first rent payment is due. Any renewal options should also be noted.

Rent Payments

The three basic types of lease are as follows:

1. *Gross Leases:* the landlord pays all operating expenses, although the tenants pick up certain expenses above an agreed amount (called an expense stop).
2. *Net Leases:* the tenant pays some operating expenses. Terms such as net, net-net, and triple net have varying meanings, depending on the market, but more "nets" means the tenant is paying more expenses.
3. *Absolute Net:* the tenant pays all operating expenses, including such things as structural maintenance and management fees. In some cases, even leasing commissions may be amortized over the lease term. These are also called bond leases, because the landlord has, in essence, a bond, and merely needs to collect interest.

It is important to clearly understand exactly how rental income and tenant contributions for expenses are to be paid, because there are considerable variances, even within a given market.

Base (or Minimum) Rent   Base rent is the initial charge for the space itself, calculated as a rate per square foot per month or year. Penalties for late rent payment should always be specified.

Escalations   Escalations are built-in automatic annual increases of the base rent, generally based upon some widely published government economic index, such as the CPI. If the CPI goes up three percent, then base rent goes up three percent for the next year. However, in the unlikely event the index dropped, rent would not go down.

Percentage Rent   Percentage rent is typical in retail leases, and is paid in addition to base rent. Usually, it represents a percentage of the tenant's sales over a specified amount. It is important to state clearly what constitutes "sales" and what means the landlord has to verify same.

Tenant Contributions   Tenant contributions represent the tenant's payments for operating expenses. The most important items to be paid by the tenant are cleaning, real estate taxes, insurance, and utilities; because these are major cost factors, they have been known to increase rapidly, and they are generally out of the landlord's control. For shopping centers and mixed use properties, common area maintenance (CAM) is also vital, because common areas are usually large and there is heavy public use of these facilities. These are typically prorated among the tenants on the basis of the portion of the total square footage occupied by each tenant.

It is essential that the specific operating expenses to be reimbursed by the tenant be clearly defined. The method of reimbursement must be stated clearly as well. Usually, it is the quotient of the tenant's space, as defined in the lease, divided by the rentable area in the entire building, then multiplied by the total expenses payable by that tenant for each year. Obviously, it is desirable if the denominator of that fraction is only the rented space in the building; otherwise, the landlord must pay all expenses accounted for by vacant space.

Additional Rent   The lease should stipulate that any payments due from the tenant for any reason (especially including reimbursement of tenant improvement costs) are considered additional rent. It is much easier to recover delinquent rent payments through legal means, and eviction becomes a remedy. Otherwise, recovery via a civil suit can be time-consuming and costly.

Concessions   Concessions should be spelled out precisely. Most common types include specified months of free rent, payments by the landlord for above-average tenant improvements, assuming the tenant's relocation or parking costs, buying the tenant's existing lease, and rights of first refusal on adjacent space. The important thing to understand is how the property's cash flow will be affected, particularly on rent concessions, and the financing the landlord may seek to pay for the tenant's improvements.

Prepaid Rent and/or Rental Offsets   Prepaid rent and/or rental offsets should be defined and clearly stated as to amount and expiration date, if appli-cable.

Purpose or Use   Purpose or use of the demised premises should always be clearly stated, and the analyst must consider conflicts with restrictions in other leases at the same property, or activities that would cause serious problems for other tenants. An obvious example is leasing space to a massage parlor in a prestigious office building.

Tenant Improvements   Responsibilities should be spelled out in detail, including payments by landlord and tenant. Normally, all tenant improvements become property of the landlord. Anything to remain tenant's property when he or she vacates should be clearly stipulated. Sometimes a landlord agrees to pay the front end costs in exchange for a higher rent, but this should be analyzed carefully, because it is only for the term of the lease and does not affect the intrinsic value of the space. The investor should value base rent from that space the same as comparable space in the property.

Maintenance, Utilities, Equipment Use, and Service

The lease should define a number of conditions for maintenance, utilities, and equipment. For instance, if the landlord pays utilities, limits on use should be set. If the tenant has special HVAC requirements, the tenant's responsibilities related to them should be laid out in detail. The landlord should have the right to service HVAC and elevators at specific times and should not be liable for equipment failure until reasonable time has passed for restoration.

The tenant's obligations related to repairs should be clear to ensure they maintain their own space in good order. The tenant's rights to alter the leased space must also be carefully defined.

Damage or Destruction

This clause stipulates rights and obligations in the event space is damaged or destroyed by casualty. The important items from the investor's point of view are the following:

■   The tenant cannot cancel the lease or sue the landlord for a breach of the lease if the tenant's space is damaged, if the landlord abates rent during restoration and agrees to restore in a reasonable time.

- At its option, the landlord may terminate the lease if damage is extensive and restoration is not economically viable. The tenant should not be permitted to share in the insurance proceeds if the landlord has paid for the policy.

- If the parties have mutually waived their rights of subrogation, the insurers must acknowledge this.

Condemnation

This clause stipulates rights and obligations in the event access roads, parking, or structural space is taken by eminent domain. The important items from the investor's point of view are as follows:

- The tenant cannot cancel the lease or sue the landlord for a breach of the lease if the taking occurs, as long as the landlord restores access or parking, and/or replacement space for the tenant, and agrees to restore in a reasonable time.

- At its option, the landlord may terminate the lease if taking is extensive and restoration is not economically viable.

- If the lease permits termination because of the extent of the taking, the tenant should not be permitted any share of the condemnation proceeds, although the tenant may be permitted, at its own expense, to join the landlord in a protest against the size of the award and seek increased proceeds because of its loss of leasehold value. The landlord should have no further obligation to the tenant because of the taking.

Substitute Premises

The landlord should also have the right to require the tenant to move to substitute premises of equal quality should an adjacent tenant want to expand. Of course, the landlord would pay moving costs and abate rent until the tenant was restored in new space.

Subordination

Most investors want the tenant to subordinate the lease to the investor's mortgage so that, in the event of foreclosure, the investor has the right to terminate an onerous lease.

Estoppel Certificates

A tenant estoppel certificate is a statement setting out the major terms of the tenant's lease and certifies that no events of default exist under the lease. Tenant estoppel certificates from all existing tenants are required by most investors prior to loan funding, and with the submission of new leases for approval during the loan term. Many form leases require the tenant to provide an estoppel within a short time frame (usually ten days) at the landlord's request.

Inspection of Premises

The landlord must have the right to inspect the premises at reasonable hours to make repairs, ensure compliance with use clauses, make safety inspections, show the space if tenant is leaving, post notices, and detect if the tenant is having operating problems.

Defaults

Conditions of tenant default, both monetary and non-monetary, should be clearly defined, along with remedies for the landlord. Right to restore and bill tenant (as additional rent) is important if the tenant neglects to comply with the lease terms or repair anything that may result in economic, health, or safety problems, or creates a liability for the landlord from covenants in another lease. Recovery of damages caused by the tenants and the right to remove the tenant's property and re-rent space should be included.

Landlord's Special Obligations

The landlord's special obligations, usually negotiated because there are some unusual circumstances or a strong tenant, should be listed in the abstract and carefully reviewed. The investor may have to live with them as well, unless the lease is subordinate to the loan.

Causes for Abatement of Rent

Causes for abatement of rent should be listed specifically in the abstract and taken into consideration in the underwriting if applicable.

Causes for Termination by Tenant

Causes for termination by tenant should be listed specifically in the abstract, and also taken into consideration in the underwriting.

Purchase Option

The purchase option by the tenant should be highlighted, if it exists, with terms and conditions clearly defined. A tenant purchase option is not acceptable to most investors, and if such exists in a lease, the investor will require it be subordinated to its lien.

■ Shopping Center Leases

The following provisions (except the exclusive use and radius clauses) should appear in all shopping center leases, primarily to make the center more profitable and ease efficient operation:

Operating Hours

The operating hours stipulate minimum hours and days of the week that the tenant must be open for business, to maximize the center's drawing power.

Continuous Occupancy

Continuous occupancy requires a tenant to remain in occupancy for the entire lease term, rather than paying minimum rent on an empty store. Default should give the landlord a remedy to accelerate the rent and evict the tenant.

Continuous Operation

Continuous operation requires the tenant to maintain the store fully stocked with inventory at the same levels as similar stores in the area.

Merchant's Association

The tenant is required to join the merchant's association, pay stipulated dues, and support its advertising efforts.

Advertising and Graphics

The landlord controls all the tenants' signs; exterior graphics, including signs in store windows; and on-premises advertising, including noise audible outside the store. The entire center should have standard graphics.

Parking Regulations

The landlord must retain complete rights to control parking by tenant employees and times and locations of tenant deliveries. Landlord should have the right to tow improperly parked cars.

Exclusive Use Clause

Strong tenants may negotiate hard for language that forbids the landlord from leasing space to competitive businesses or stores that sell even some of the goods that tenant carries. Obviously, this should be resisted, or carefully drafted, to minimize limits on landlord's flexibility.

Radius Clauses

Radius clauses require agreement from the landlord that he or she will not lease space to competitive tenants not only at the subject property but also at any other commercial real estate the landlord may own within a defined radius of the subject property. This could cause a problem for an investor if he or she happened to take back the subject property and own other competing centers nearby as well. At the least, the investor should be exempted from this provision.

It is important to note that both exclusive use and radius clauses have been the subject of litigation recently and may be prohibited if there is clear evidence of restraint of trade.

◼ Other Business Issues

A number of other business conditions should be in the lease to make management's job easier, but are not critical from the investor's standpoint. Among them are the following:

Sign Restrictions

Sign restrictions are particularly important in shopping centers, but may be needed in office buildings as well. The landlord should have the right to approve all exterior graphics and signage. Ideally, the landlord should ensure that all signage is uniform and tastefully done.

Name Change

The landlord should have the right to change the building's name, particularly if the building is named for a major tenant and that tenant leaves. This will protect the landlord from complaints by tenants who may not like a new name (particularly if it's that of a competitor).

Air, Light, and View Rights

The lease should be clear that these are retained by the landlord. In the age of the lawsuit, the landlord may be sued because of external environment problems beyond its control (like new construction blocking light or a view).

Rules and Regulations

The rules and regulations of the building should be attached as an exhibit to the lease.

■ Legal Issues

The following clauses should be present, but contents and drafting are subject to legal review:

Environmental Hazards Indemnification

This indemnifies the landlord against liability for environmental hazards created, knowingly or unknowingly, by the activities of the tenant.

Hold Harmless

A hold harmless clause should be present, protecting the landlord from liability for damages due to the acts of the tenant, its visitors, agents, or employees. It further states that if damages result from the tenant's negligence in the common areas, that the tenant will agree to hold the landlord harmless. A good lease provision will require the tenant to take out liability insurance in a specified amount and name the landlord as additional insured. In addition, the tenant should be restricted from any activity that will increase the landlord's fire insurance premium.

Strict Performance

Strict performance clauses stipulate that the landlord's waiver of one default does not constitute waiver of any other.

Assignment and Subletting

Assignment and subletting should be prohibited without the landlord's express written consent, although tenants always try for a "reasonableness" clause. If assignment/subletting is permitted, the landlord should require that there are no events of default under the tenant's lease, that the original tenant remain fully liable for all obligations of the lease, and that the landlord has the right to review and approve the complete sublease/assignment agreement.

Compliance with Laws

The landlord's obligation to comply with laws affecting real property does not shift to the tenant upon execution of a lease. It is thus appropriate for the tenant to agree to compliance, at the tenant's own expense. The rule of thumb is that if compliance relates to tenant's business, or a need is caused by tenant's business, the tenant pays.

Notice

A mechanism must exist for the landlord and tenant to provide legal notice to each other. Address and time requirement stipulations are required.

Attorney's Fees

The tenant should agree to pay the landlord's attorney's fees and court costs for any action taken by the landlord to enforce the lease.

Surrender of Possession

This clause stipulates the tenant's obligations at lease termination to leave or remove certain improvements made by the tenant, and leave the space as it was found, normal wear and tear excepted.

Holding Over

This clause covers the landlord's rights in the event the tenant fails to vacate the space as of the termination date of the lease. Penalty rent is often required, and eviction is a remedy. The tenant must also continue to abide by the other terms of the lease, and the landlord's additional remedies for default are listed.

■ Monitoring Credit Instruments

Monitoring credit instruments is an important function of commercial real estate servicing. If they are not properly monitored, security or remedies to protect security can be weakened. Credit instruments generally include loan guarantee agreements, letters of credit, and completion escrow arrangements. These are discussed in more detail below.

Loan Guarantee Agreements

Often a loan guarantee agreement is drawn as additional security for granting a commercial real estate mortgage. The agreement may be part of the note or a separate document; if it is the latter, it should be kept with the loan documents. Because the guarantor is insuring a portion or all of the mortgage, it is important that he or she be aware of situations that may affect the terms of the mortgage and note. Also, the financial condition of the guarantor should be monitored. This will enable the loan administrator to know that the guarantor still possesses value. The servicing file, as well as any abstract of the file, should reflect that there is a guarantee and that the guarantor's consent must be obtained for any loan modifications. Notice provisions of the guarantee agreement must be complied with at all times. A demand on the guarantee may be required if the borrower defaults. Legal counsel should be retained to make the demand.

A tickler system, whether manual or automated, should be utilized to ensure that the loan administrator is aware of the guarantor and follows the notice provisions of the agreement. This system will notify the loan administrator of the need to notify the guarantor and also follow up on obtaining financial statements of the guarantor.

Letters of Credit

To enhance a commercial mortgage agreement, a letter of credit may be required by the investor and held until various requirements are met. The loan administrator needs to be aware of these letters of credit and possible required extensions and to realize that to enforce them, demand must be made before they expire. This awareness can be fostered by establishing a tickler file that lists the expiration dates of letters of credit and by making this list available to the loan administrator in ample time to take action before the expiration. The loan administrator must also be aware under what terms the letters of credit can be released or must be extended.

Holdbacks/Completion Escrows

At times investors will escrow monies for the eventual benefit of the borrower with the understanding that the funds will be released upon certain conditions. For example, the escrows may be set aside for rental achievements, property repairs, completion of construction, or environmental problems. A written agreement covering the escrows is necessary, and the monies should be placed in an account that is separate from escrow accounts used to accrue monies for payment of real estate taxes and/or insurance. Sometimes the monies will be stipulated to be held with a third party escrow agent. Often the agreement will stipulate that the monies be placed in interest-bearing accounts and/or money access accounts, with the interest accruing for the benefit of the borrower. The agreement usually provides that after a fixed period of time, if the conditions for which the escrows were established are not met, the monies will either revert to the investor or be applied against the outstanding principal balance of the mortgage. If the borrower requests the escrowed funds, the loan administrator must make sure that all conditions have been met. Before releasing funds, the loan administrator should obtain approval from the investor.

Again, establishing a tickler file will aid in monitoring these monies and the agreements.

■ Summary

This Chapter covered the importance of analyzing financial statements to determine if the property is performing in accordance with pro forma statements. Income, expenses, and the computation of net operating income and debt coverage ratio are areas requiring special attention.

In most types of commercial real estate, lease income provides the bulk of revenues available to service the mortgage loan. For rental properties, the items in a lease that need to be scrutinized were covered as well as the special considerations necessary to protect revenues generated by shopping center leases.

For legal clauses that are generally incorporated into leases, the content should be subjected to legal review. Most legal clauses deal with environmental issues, compliance with laws, and landlord-tenant rights.

Finally, the credit instruments used in the servicing of commercial real estate were covered. Instruments such as loan guarantee agreements, letters of credit, holdbacks, and completion escrows help to protect and secure commercial real estate and, as such, need to be monitored on a regular basis.

■ Chapter 5 Review Questions

1. The financial analysis of an income-producing property is executed by a certified public accountant.

   a. True

   b. False

2. Which item is important to scrutinize when analyzing sources of income?

   a. Leases expiring within the next 90 days

   b. Leases expiring within the next 12 months

   c. The ratio of annual income to current interest rate

   d. The ratio of lease payments to current interest rate

3. Check off five items used in the evaluation of a lease.

   _____ Defaults

   _____ Demised premises

   _____ Rent payments

   _____ Tenant contributions

   _____ Exclusive use clause

   _____ Condemnation clause

   _____ Continuous occupancy

4. Which is *NOT* a common type of lease concession?

   a. Prepaid rent

   b. Assumption of relocation costs

   c. Payments for above average improvements

   d. Non-escalation of rent payments for up to three years

5. Check five provisions found in shopping center leases.

   _____ Radius clause

   _____ Parking regulations

   _____ Substitute premises

   _____ Continuous occupancy

   _____ Merchant's association

   _____ Advertising and graphics

   _____ Landlord's special obligations

6. Who is responsible for controlling the signs, exterior graphics, and on-premises advertising at a shopping center?

   a. Lender

   b. Tenant

   c. Landlord

   d. Leasing agent

7. Match the description to the appropriate clause.

   _____ Holding over

   _____ Hold harmless

   _____ Strict performance

   a. Protects landlord from damages due to tenants, visitors, agents, or employees

   b. Covers landlord's rights if tenants fail to vacate premises on their termination date

   c. Stipulates that landlord's waiver of one default does not constitute waiver of any other

8. Which clause protects a landlord against liability for environmental hazards created by the activities of tenants?

   a. Holdback

   b. Hold harmless

   c. Environmental damage or destruction

   d. Environmental hazards indemnification

9. Which is not a credit instrument?
    a. Holdback
    b. Letter of credit
    c. Re-conveyance
    d. Completion escrows
    e. Loan guarantee agreement

10. Whose consent must be obtained if a modification is made on a loan with a loan guarantee agreement?
    a. Trustee
    b. Guarantor
    c. Equity agent
    d. Title insurance agent

6

Property Inspections

Upon completion of this chapter, you should be able to

■ identify the physical aspects of a property inspection;

■ recognize the neighborhood factors and market trends used in a property inspection; and

■ ascertain the key elements in a property inspection report.

■ Introduction

When the phrase was coined, "a picture is worth a thousand words," property inspections may not have been in the author's mind, but the phrase is certainly fitting. Of all the areas of commercial loan administration, visual inspections of the security property reveal the greatest wealth of information in the shortest amount of time.

Of course, the reason for routine scheduled property inspections is to determine the property's current physical condition, occupancy status, and significant changes that have occurred since the last visit. Deterioration of the property, loss of tenants, and a decline in the surrounding neighborhood make the loan less secure and reduce the chances of selling the property to recover the outstanding debt. The security property's physical condition is one factor used to determine the quality of the investment. An analysis of neighborhoods and market trends is a valuable source of information. This data provides information about whether an area is declining, improving, or staying the same. Once the necessary information is collected, the loan administrator prepares an inspection report incorporating this information.

■ Property Inspection Parameters

Physical Aspects of Property

The servicing agreement between the investor and the correspondent generally determines the inspection requirements. As a general rule, investors require annual inspections of their properties. More frequent inspections may be required in the case of a loan default or pending foreclosure. The mortgagor's loan documents usually grant the investor the right to perform such periodic inspections of the security property.

Several practical tips can help the loan administrator organize a physical inspection of the property. The loan administrator should take photographs of each full side of each building in a shopping center, office complex, or industrial warehouse. In large apartment complexes or other multi-building properties, enough photographs should be taken to give a fair representation of the property as a whole. Photographs should also be taken of significant changes, such as new construction and deferred maintenance.

Memories are selective and fade quickly, so it is wise to take notes during or immediately after observing the property. The loan administrator should record actual observations and avoid making assumptions. As the "eyes and ears" for the investor, the loan administrator must forward accurate, factual information. Vague speculation about particular causes of deferred maintenance or tenant loss should be avoided. Instead, the observed conditions of deferred maintenance or tenant loss should be discussed with the mortgagor to determine the actual causes. The investor's inspection form and a current rent roll should be in hand so all information required by the investor can be gathered on the spot.

Each property type has unique attributes. When inspecting office buildings, the loan administrator should note atriums, elaborate lobbies, interior shops and restaurants, and covered parking. For shopping centers, the loan administrator should note street access, adequacy of parking and exterior lighting, and visibility from the street. Apartments may offer a wide range of amenities such as pools, exercise rooms, laundry rooms (which may be additional income for the property) and covered parking, which should be noted. A check of the current rental quotes for the various apartment sizes may be useful later in an economic analysis of the property. Industrial properties may have front or rear loading docks. Perhaps there are equipment or vehicle wash facilities or truck scales. The aspects of the property that make it more valuable or less secure to the investor are of key interest.

Next, with rent roll in hand, the loan administrator should note any changes in the actual tenant occupancy. The loan administrator should note whether or not any of the tenants have "Liquidation" or "Fire Sale" signs in their windows. If the property displays visible leasing or "For Information" signs, this should be indicated. The loan administrator may wish to briefly speak with a representative number of tenants and gather any tenant comments.

To prevent disturbing the tenants, it is strongly recommended that the mortgagor or property manager accompany the loan administrator during the inspection. At the very least, tenants should be notified by the mortgagor of the scheduled inspection prior to the loan administrator's visit. The property manager can answer many questions about property condition and tenant occupancy on the spot. The loan administrator should ask questions but be cordial, not demanding, and listen well.

The loan administrator may meet with the same person each year or each scheduled visit, so a good working rapport will keep the information flowing.

As environmental problems continue to be an issue, the loan administrator should report any obvious or suspect abuses in the written report to the investor. Items of concern may include obvious dumping of trash, liquids, barrels, or materials; evidence of stressed vegetation and stained soil; leaking or damaged storage barrels; and environmental red flag tenants, such as an auto repairshop or a dry-cleaning facility. If there are suspect abuses and the investor feels it is warranted, a qualified professional should perform an environmental inspection. The loan administrator should never represent itself as an environmental or hazardous waste expert unless that is indeed the case. Also, the loan administrator should avoid drawing unconfirmed conclusions and may want to include environmental disclaimer language in the inspection report.

After the loan administrator has observed and noted the physical aspects of the property and the status of the tenants, his or her attention should turn to the neighborhood and market trends.

■ Neighborhood and Market Trends

Composition of the surrounding area and an estimate of the percentages of residential, commercial, industrial, farmland, and raw land should be noted. The loan administrator should note if the area is primarily urban, suburban, or rural. The activity in the area such as new construction, traffic congestion, or lack of traffic and neighborhood vacancies should be noted, as well as the nearby visible competition to the subject property. The loan administrator should get an overall impression for whether the area is generally declining, improving, changing, or simply remaining stable.

In addition to the data from the site visit, there are other documents that can improve the accuracy and depth of the inspection report. An accurate, up-to-date property survey of the land and building is very helpful. It will not only depict what the security property is, such as whether the entire building is included or if the pad sites should be excluded, but it may note parking spaces and second floor construction. The loan documents and correspondence on prior inspections of the property may reveal areas requiring special attention or follow-up. Side-letter agreements, special loan covenants, holdbacks for repairs, etc., would be well worth noting before the visit to the property. Often one inspection trip can serve more than one purpose.

■ Preparation of the Inspection Report

Preparing the written inspection report is not as difficult a task as may be anticipated from viewing the stacks of papers, photographs, and documents collected. Most investors have a form report they prefer, giving the loan administrator a starting point for organizing the data. Once the initial report is completed, the loan administrator simply has to update it each year. Photographs should be arranged and organized to "tell the story" of the property to the investor. Often it is useful to start with the front entrance to the building or complex and perhaps an identification sign and then show the remaining sides of the building. Next include the interior photographs, the amenities, or special quality photographs of the property, and then end with the photographs of deferred maintenance. The photographs and the current (and updated) rent roll should be attached to the inspection report.

The inspection report should include the actual date the property was inspected, current loan information, the current condition of the exterior and interior of the buildings in a checklist fashion, and commentary to give a general overview of the property's condition and to elaborate on deferred maintenance.

Lastly, the mortgagor should be informed in writing of maintenance items requiring attention. Now is a good time to conduct a lease review to verify that current lease information is on file. Missing lease documents or information should be requested from the mortgagor. The loan administrator is advised to monitor the situation until the maintenance problems are cured and outstanding lease documents are collected.

The periodic visual inspection of the security property is certainly one of the most important tasks of loan servicing. This information collected on a timely basis can give the investor advance notice of potential loan defaults. It is much easier to deal with the beginning of a relatively small problem up-front than a full-blown problem of a property in decline. The property inspection report brings the property to the investor without requiring the investor to leave the office. The investor and the loan administrator both know that when it comes to evaluating a property's potential decline or success, a photograph really is worth a thousand words.

■ Summary

This Chapter stressed the importance of property inspections in revealing an enormous amount of information in a relatively short amount of time. The inspection begins with an assessment of the physical dimensions of a property. Taking photographs of the property insures that the property as a whole is fairly represented and determines if the condition of the property is adversely affecting the quality of the investment.

The composition of the neighborhood and its activity in new construction traffic assessment and vacancies provide useful information about the property. A review of market trends helps the loan administrator to assess the health of an area—whether it is declining, improving, or remaining stable.

After the physical inspection, the neighborhood analysis, and the review of market trends, the information is put into an inspection report. Most investors have a form report that is used for such inspections.

■ Chapter 6 Review Questions

1. Which area of commercial loan administration reveals the greatest wealth of information in the shortest amount of time?

   a. Appraisals

   b. Landlord files

   c. Lease documents

   d. Property inspections

2. Which of the following is not a "red flag" tenant?

   a. Photo lab

   b. Shoe store

   c. Dry cleaner

   d. Auto repair shop

3. In addition to data from the site visit, which document can help to improve the accuracy and depth of the inspection report?

   a. Land plat

   b. Property survey

   c. MLS description

   d. Comparable assessments

4. Which is *NOT* a document that might be inspected when assessing a neighborhood?

   a. All risk coverage

   b. Special loan covenants

   c. Side-letter agreements

   d. Holdbacks for repairs

5. The property inspection report should include all of the following *EXCEPT*

   a. current loan information.

   b. actual date of property inspection.

   c. turnover rates of homes in the defined area.

   d. current condition of interior and exterior of building.

6. When organizing photographs of a building, number the steps in order of their suggested arrangement.

   _____ Front entrance

   _____ Interior photographs

   _____ Deferred maintenance

   _____ Sides of the building

   _____ Amenities or special quality photographs

Transfer of Ownership

learning objectives

Upon completion of this chapter, you should be able to

- determine the initial events in a request for sale or transfer of property;

- identify the information required in a transfer of ownership form; and

- recognize the components in a payoff request.

■ Introduction

The sale or transfer of income property, subject to the mortgage, requires extensive review by the loan administrator, regardless of whether or not the mortgage requires the prior written consent of the investor. Loan administrators need to be in a position to re-underwrite the transaction and provide the investor with substantial documentation and their recommendations. Loan administrators should keep in mind their fiduciary responsibility not to divulge information to a prospective purchaser without the borrower's permission.

Generally, by the time the sales contract is executed, it becomes crucial to obtain the written consents required in the mortgage. However, loan administrators cannot allow a borrower to be overdemanding about turnaround time on approvals, and they must clearly convey the documentation that is required to review the request.

After the documents are reviewed, the loan administrator advises the borrower of the results of the review and requests information concerning the sales contract and prospective purchaser. If the request is approved, the investor may also require the borrower to provide information on the loan, insurance coverage, contact information, and identification numbers.

When an investor accepts a transfer request, the loan administrator sends the borrower a transfer of ownership form to complete along with additional information requirements. There are suggested payoff request procedures to insure that a variety of situations can be addressed.

■ Request for the Sale or Transfer of Property

Request in Writing

If the current borrower contacts the loan administrator by telephone with a request for sale or transfer of the property subject to the mortgage, the loan administrator should advise the borrower that the request must be made in writing. The written notification should explain the transaction in detail, including the following:

- Timing.
- Identity of all parties.
- Specific commentary regarding liability.

After receiving the letter, the loan administrator begins the process of reviewing the following information.

- Determine whether the mortgage documents provide for a due-on-sale clause, prior written consent of transfer, a transfer fee, or personal guarantees. If the mortgage does not require written consent, but the borrower requests it, ensure that the borrower complies as if consent were required.
- Determine whether the state laws uphold due-on-sale provisions.
- Determine whether the management company will continue or be replaced.
- Review the past year's loan history to determine whether payments, taxes, insurance, operating statements, and UCC information are current and satisfactory.
- Review the latest property inspection report to determine whether there are structural or maintenance deficiencies in the property.

The loan administrator should then advise the borrower of the results of the review and request the following information:

- Copy of executed purchase and sales contract; if the contract is assignable, obtain the name of the purchasing entity
- Resumé of the proposed purchaser's experience and expertise as it relates to the property

Request the following if the proposed purchaser is an individual, or group of individuals:

- Current (within the past 90 days) signed financial statement from each individual involved
- Credit information (e.g., bank, business references)

If the proposed purchaser is a legal entity, get the following:

- Copy of agreement forming the entity (articles of incorporation, partnership agreements, etc.)
- The entity's audited financial statement, including at least the past two years operating statement and balance sheets

- Current and past two years' and pro forma operating statement, occupancy level, and rent roll on the subject property and an explanation of any extraordinary items on the financials
- Short and long-term management plan addressing capital improvements, expansion, and remedies for any current problems

Investor Requirements

If a request for transfer is approved, the investor may also require the specific information listed below.

- Copy of recorded deed
- UCC-3 statement, when required
- An appropriate insurance coverage as required by the investor with proper mortgagee and cancellation clauses
- Name, address, and telephone number of a contact person
- Billing address
- Notice address
- Assumption agreement
- Tax identification number—completed W-9

After all documentation is received, the loan administrator should review it thoroughly and make a recommendation to the investor. If the investor approves the transfer for a certain fee, the loan administrator should require the fee immediately and advise the borrower that the approval is subject to the receipt of the fee. Because of the time involved in reviewing a deal, many loan administrators and investors require a reasonable nonrefundable processing fee. This fee is not necessarily the entire transfer fee charge; the borrower should be told that the investor may require an additional fee, principal paydown, and/or modification of the loan documents as to maturity, interest rate, late charges, grace periods, and amount of monthly payments.

This fee should be placed in escrow until closing. Upon receipt of the fee and approval by the investor, the loan administrator should send a commitment letter to the borrower describing the requirements of the investor to effectuate the transfer and supply the necessary estoppel information. If the investor denies the transfer request, the loan administrator should send the borrower a letter describing the reasons of the denial.

Transfer of Ownership Form

Required Information

A transfer of ownership form is usually completed, where appropriate, by the loan administrator and then sent to the borrower to be completed and returned with the requested information.

The following must be submitted with this application:

- A written request from the borrower outlining in detail the transaction, including timing, details of parties, liability, and specific consents requested

- Processing fee
- Copy of an executed Purchase and Sale Agreement
- Last two to three years' income and expense statement, current year-to-date and pro forma statements
- Certified rent roll of present occupancy, including terms, rates, options, etc. (if multi-tenant property other than apartments). For apartments: breakdown of units, rent per unit, concessions
- Complete background information on the proposed buyer, including personal financial statements, credit references, resume, etc.
- New UCC-1 financing statements prepared for signature and containing the following wording:

  (Buyer) does hereby grant and convey to Investor Insurance Company a security interest in the property described in a Mortgage and Security Agreement dated (Date of Execution) between (Original Owner) and Investor Life Insurance Company for the purpose of securing the payment of a Note executed by (Original Owner) on (Date of Execution) and does hereby expressly and unconditionally assume all of the covenants and obligations of (Original Owner) as set forth in said Mortgage and Security Agreement.

- UCC-11 Chattel Searches on the present owner and proposed buyer from the County Recorder's Office and/or Secretary of State where the property is located (in accordance with state law)
- Background of new management company including past and present experiences
- New inspection should be done by loan administrator
- Inspection on one or more of other properties owned by proposed buyer

Additional Elements

If this request is approved, the following additional information must be provided:

- At or prior to the closing—a new insurance binder evidencing Fire and Extended coverage in accordance with the insurance requirements of the loan as contained in the original loan documents. The insurance carrier must be notified of any second mortgagee, and their second lien position *must* be so noted on the insurance certificate.
- Within five (5) days after the closing—notification that the transaction as approved has closed and the effective date thereof.

■ Payoff Requests

Income property mortgages are entered into for a fixed period of time with the investor expecting to receive a stated rate of return. To protect this investment, the mortgage will usually contain a lock-in provision. The provision is for a specific term and will permit a prepayment after that time with a prepayment premium.

For example, a typical lock-in provision may state that the mortgage is locked in for a period of three years and may be repaid beginning in the fourth year with a prepayment premium. The terms may also provide that the mortgage is locked in for the term of the mortgage, especially if the term is of a short duration, such as three to five years. On more seasoned loans that were made with long-term maturities, such as 20 years to 25 years, a typical lock-in provision might be for 10 years and provide that the mortgage may be repaid after that time, with prepayment premiums that may decrease each year over the next several years until the mortgage reaches the point where it may be paid in full without a prepayment premium. Notwithstanding the mortgage provisions, mortgagors occasionally request that they be permitted to prepay the mortgage and may also request a waiver of the prepayment premium.

Payoff Procedures

When a request is received for a payoff statement, it is suggested that the following steps be taken:

- Review loan documents to determine
  1. if the loan can be prepaid,
  2. if a prepayment premium is due,
  3. if written notice is required of the borrower within a specified period, and
  4. any other terms or conditions which affect a payoff or prepayment. Special care should be taken to determine if the loan documents have been changed or the loan renewed, extended, or otherwise modified so as to change the original terms of the loan regarding these matters.
- When calculating the amount of additional consideration that is owed to the lender due to the prepayment of principal on the loan, the servicer should base the calculations on the unpaid balance unless the loan documents provide for the calculation to be based on the original amount of the loan. If the documents provide for a partial prepayment without payment of a premium, this calculation should be made prior to the calculation of the premium. The servicer should determine the amount of the prepayment premium and submit the entire payoff figure for the lender's approval. The prepayment premium should be shown separately on a mortgage loan collection report when payment in full is reported to the lender. Any and all such funds collected are the property of the lender and should be wire transferred to the lender according to their wiring instructions.
- Review the investor's requirements to determine if the investor provides for any deviation from the mortgage terms.
- Prepare a statement modified as necessary for particular loans, including calculations of prepayment premiums, interest, late charges, and unexpired written notice term, if applicable. The lender's approval must be obtained unless there are specific instructions from the lender to the contrary.
- Advise the mortgagor and/or any other requesting parties involved as to the specific mortgage terms.
- Inform the mortgagor of the investor's decision to accept or decline prepayment along with any conditions the investor may want to establish, and give a definite time frame for granting the approval. In times of volatile interest rate changes, prepayment premiums may change quickly because of reinvestment yields, and mortgagors need to know that the prepayment premium quoted is valid for only a fixed time period.
- The mortgage may stipulate that a lock-in provision or a prepayment premium may be imposed, but legal rulings in specific areas of the country may

prohibit charging the premium. This matter should be conveyed to the investor and to the investor's legal counsel for a decision. Loan administrators should not attempt to render legal opinions but may of course advise the investor of any precedents.

■ Borrowers are often anxious to obtain payoff figures to meet a preset closing deadline. Servicers should make every attempt to be sensitive to those needs. If this process will delay the closing beyond the borrower's requested date, the borrower or their closing attorneys should be advised and the lender should be apprised of the situation.

■ Before payoff information is sent out, determine if the borrower has made the request in writing or has authorized its release. For example, occasionally real estate practitioners or prospective purchasers will ask for payoff information in order to determine their offer to the borrower. Care should always be taken that information is released based on a request from the borrower. Instructions on the use of escrowed funds must also be in writing from the borrower.

■ All payoff statements must be reviewed and approved by management prior to its release to the borrower (or representative). Two managers must approve a commercial payoff. Residential loan payoffs must be approved by one manager. These requirements may vary with each servicer's in-house policies.

■ Record mortgage release documents and UCC terminations if needed after return by lender, cancel original unrecorded documents, and forward all to the borrower.

■ Unused funds in escrow should be returned as instructed by the borrower subject to the following: Upon foreclosure or sale of the note by a lender, care must be taken to determine ownership of escrowed funds from the lender or its attorney.

■ Review file to assure all items were properly handled including escrowed funds, and check computer system to confirm removal of the loan.

■ Files on paid-off loans should be placed in the "paid in full" section in the file room. The time required to maintain these files varies with each state and servicer.

■ Summary

This Chapter covered the procedures in a transfer of ownership of income property. To activate the process, the borrower notifies the loan administrator in writing of his or her request for the sale or transfer of property subject to the mortgage. Upon receiving the letter, the administrator requests information from the borrower on the property and the prospective purchaser.

If the request is approved, the investor will generally require specific information from the borrower. This may include loan documents, UCC statements, insurance coverage, contact information, and tax identifiers.

If the transfer is accepted, the borrower completes a transfer of ownership form and submits additional information and processing fees. Once this documentation is processed, methods of payoff are addressed. The specific steps in the payoff procedure help to guarantee that a multitude of situations can be covered.

■ Chapter 7 Review Questions

1. If the request for the sale or transfer of property is favorably reviewed, check the four items that may be requested of the borrower.

   _____ New UCC financing statements

   _____ Credit information on purchaser

   _____ Resumé of proposed purchaser

   _____ Copy of executed sales contract

   _____ Certified rent roll of present occupancy

   _____ Short-term and long-term management plans of purchaser

2. To whom do borrowers send their written requests for the sale or transfer of property?

   a. Investor

   b. Trustee

   c. Loan administrator

   d. Transfer or sale agent

3. Along with the transfer of ownership form, a borrower must submit income and expense statements for the past

   a. year.

   b. 2 to 3 years.

   c. 5 years.

   d. 10 years.

4. What is *NOT* submitted by the borrower with a transfer of ownership form?

   a. Processing fee

   b. Payoff lock-in provision

   c. Background information on the proposed buyer

   d. Copy of an executed Purchase and Sale Agreement

5. Check off the four items in a loan file that are reviewed by a loan administrator upon receipt of a request for payoff.

   _____ If the loan can be prepaid

   _____ The currency of UCC statements

   _____ If the deed of trust is assumable

   _____ The existence of due dates for prepayment penalties

   _____ Any miscellaneous terms and conditions that may affect payoff or prepayment

   _____ If written notice within a specified time period is required of the borrower

6. Legal rules may prohibit any prepayment premiums of lock-in provisions stipulated in a mortgage.

   a. True

   b. False

Partial Releases and Easements

---

learning objectives

Upon completion of this chapter, you should be able to

■ ascertain the role of partial releases and easements in commercial real estate;

■ identify the considerations in a request for release; and

■ recognize the items required in an easement request.

■ Introduction

A partial release of the mortgage can be defined as the release of a portion of the property from the lien of a mortgage and/or deed of trust. The following two factors should be kept in mind to administer this type of request:

1. A "pure" partial release is a voluntary request by the borrower with the mortgagee having a right to accept or reject the release terms.
2. A partial release under an eminent domain/condemnation principle is involuntary and is usually a result of taking powers granted to a local, state, or federal authority for the benefit of the public.

Occasionally, an easement may be associated with the release. An *easement* can be defined as an interest in the land and/or rights to the property owner entitling the beneficiary of the easement for a specific use to those rights and interest. Easements may be classified into two groups:

1. Easements of appurtenance
2. Easements in gross

■ Partial Releases

Overview

A partial release encompasses not only a release of land, but the air rights as well. Partial release requests are sometimes confused with the concept of eminent domain in condemnation proceedings. Condemnation is the taking of private property for public use under the right of eminent domain with just compensation paid the owner. It is extremely important that a request for a release be analyzed from both underwriting and economic standpoints.

A mortgagor may request a partial release of security for many reasons. The mortgagor may want to obtain a mortgage commitment from another investor and want to improve a portion of property (i.e., incumbent by a mortgage). The new investor would desire a first mortgage lien position on the land and his or her commitment would unduly require the borrower to obtain a partial release from the first lien holder mortgage. In this case, development by the mortgagor is the impetus behind the request. However, the mortgagor may well wish to sell the unimproved property to a third party for cash consideration. In that case, development by another is motivating the request. There are other situations that could compel the partial release request, and the investors should know the reason for the request in order to make the appropriate analysis.

The most important item to consider when a partial release or easement is requested is the investor's current policy guidelines on what information is required before the request can be considered. Although each situation must be analyzed on its own facts or merits, investor requirements in this area are generally similar.

Components of Partial Releases

The following items must be considered whenever a request is received:

- A written request from the borrower outlining the reasons for the land being sold or transferred and what is the intended use of the released land. Is the release being requested to handle financial difficulties, and if so, what is the intended use of the collateral being released?

- A description of the collateral proposed to be released. A diagram or survey of the property that clearly shows the partial release is important. A legal description of the parcel to be released provides additional clarification of the property being reviewed. These documents should be tied together by a short, concise narrative highlighting the important changes to the property including adjusted means of legal access to the security, geographical peculiarities, changed sidelines, and changes to the amount of parking spaces.

- Verification of the proposed transaction resulting from a release. A copy of the sales contract and/or copies of the appraisal and/or valuation reports that the borrower may have used in determining the purchase price provided as to the funds to be received by the borrower.

- Initially the loan administrator should supply to the investor a complete loan summary outlining the original loan amounts, the current balances, date closed, maturity dates, current payment status, etc.

- Property condition or general summary of the property's condition and performance over the past two years. An inspection report should be completed if the most recent report is over one year old.

- Most mortgage documents give the investor the right to apply the entire consideration reduction of the loan. If the borrower proposes to retain a portion of the consideration, request an explanation. In some cases, it may be determined that a paydown is not in the mortgagee's best interest. Therefore, disposition on the consideration paid by the borrower, if any, should be determined on a case-by-case basis.

- Determine how the partial release affects the security to the outstanding debt and what steps can be taken to correct deficiencies. Loan modifications such as rate increases and other term changes may be assessed to properly adjust for any deficiencies which may be created as a result of a partial release.

- Determine if there are any improvements or utilities located on the portion to be released. If so, what arrangements have been made to relocate them? With the partial allowed, what is the quality of access and/or visibility of the remaining property?

- Obtain the consent of the title company. A letter from the company may suffice for the investor to process the release. However, as a condition of approval, the investor should require an endorsement to the policy indicating that the continued priority of the mortgage lien is insured and the release does not adversely affect title coverage.

■ Easements

Overview

An easement of appurtenance is an interest that one owner of real property may enjoy in the real property of another. An easement of ingress/egress for the benefit of the adjacent property owner is an example. An easement in gross is a more personal interest in the real property of another. For example, utility easement may be requested to allow a switch box to be placed at one end of the property. The box may need to be removed from a location near a busy street or intersection to eliminate danger or power interruption. The objective on all easements is to preserve the investor's security as originally underwritten, ensuring that it remains in compliance with all zoning, subdivision, planned community, and development laws.

Easements are requested for three main reasons:

1. In order to lay sewer lines, electrical power lines, or gas lines running to and through the property (usually underground)
2. For ingress/egress
3. To accommodate tunnel rights between buildings, skyways, parking, etc.

They are generally created by express written agreements between the parties and specifically describe their rights, restrictions, and responsibilities and prorate the maintenance and operating expenses associated with the easement. Occasionally easements are requested to modernize an already existing system.

Easement Requirements

Like the information required of the releases above, there are other items that will be required. These include the following:

- A detailed explanation of the reason for the easement request, including a detailed explanation of the easement describing the change to the property

- A survey or diagram of the property which clearly shows the easement along with a matching legal description
- A copy of the easement agreement, right-of-way taking, or other documents formalizing the transaction
- Amount of proceeds, if any, and who will receive these benefits
- What measures, if any, to be taken to correct deficiencies of the property as a result of the easement

There may not be a cash consideration involved in the granting of an easement because there tends to be some mutual benefit to the parties. However, title company consent is absolutely essential when considering a partial release and/or easement request. Any change to the original security in which the title company insures the lien of the mortgage will necessitate its consent. Because the release will alter the legal description and the rights and obligations of the parties, thereby affecting title, without title company consent the investor may adversely impair the lien of the mortgage. In addition, changes in size and configuration of the original parcel may also affect the parcel's compliance with local laws on zoning, sideline, setback, etc. Therefore, the investor also needs a statement from a local zoning board indicating that the release will not violate these laws.

The investor should also consider parking ratio requirements and the effect on existing tenant leases when processing a release and/or easement. If the release or easement will adversely affect the desirability or functional use of the property, there is a potential danger of loss of tenancy and subsequent cash flow, thereby diminishing the borrower's ability to meet the debt service. The investor cannot rely solely on the mortgagor to address these concerns.

When considering any such request, the loan administrator should ask the question, What benefit flows to the investor if this request is granted? In answering this question, many times the alternative question of, What harm can be done to the investor if this request is granted? may automatically arise. In answering these questions, the loan administrator will gain additional insight and guidance for meaningful information to the investor for consideration of a request to grant a partial release or easement.

■ Summary

This Chapter covered the role of partial releases and easements in the real estate market. A partial release is the release of a portion of a property from the lien of a mortgage and/or deed of trust. "Pure" partial release is a voluntary request by a borrower with the mortgagee having a right to accept or reject the offer. A partial release under eminent domain is involuntary and is generally a result of taking powers granted to local, state, or federal authorities for the good of the public.

An easement is an interest in the land and/or rights to the property owner entitling the beneficiary of the easement for a specific use to those rights and interest. An easement of appurtenance is an interest that one owner of real property may enjoy in the real property of another. An easement in gross is a more personal interest in the property of another.

■ Chapter 8 Review Questions

1. What is a release of a portion of property from the lien of a mortgage or deed of trust called?

    a. Egress release

    b. Partial release

    c. Earnest release

    d. Substantiated release

2. An easement may be requested for all of the following reasons *EXCEPT*

    a. for egress.

    b. to lay sewer lines.

    c. to correct property lines.

    d. to accommodate tunnel rights.

3. In a request for partial release, an inspection report must be completed if the most recent one is over

    a. 1 year old.

    b. 18 months old.

    c. 2 years old.

    d. 3 years old.

4. Why might a mortgagor request a partial release of security?

    a. To limit tax liability

    b. To avoid seizure by the IRS

    c. To dispose of environmentally impaired property

    d. To sell unimproved property for cash consideration

5. In an easement request, to avoid impairing the lien of a mortgage, consent must be obtained from the

    a. underwriter.

    b. title company.

    c. loan administrator.

    d. county where property is located.

6. Which is not an item required in easement requests?

    a. Survey of property

    b. Amount of proceeds and distribution list

    c. Written explanation citing reasons for request

    d. Measures taken to correct deficiencies of the property

9

Commercial Property Workouts

Upon completion of this chapter, you should be able to

■ Identify the strategies to detect potential mortgage defaults;

■ recognize the sources of delinquencies and defaults;

■ determine the advantages and disadvantages of loan restructuring; and

■ ascertain the characteristics of a restructured loan.

■ Introduction

Problem commercial property loans and subsequent workout and restructuring activities are extremely labor intensive and a drain on resources. Therefore, it is incumbent upon the loan administrator to know as much about the loan portfolio as possible to identify potential problems before they result in default.

This Chapter will cover the strategies to detect defaults, sources of delinquencies and defaults, the characteristics of workouts, and the rights of a mortgagee in possession. By reviewing operating statements, tax payments, insurance coverage, physical property characteristics, and by monitoring the timeliness of debt service payments, a loan administrator can become aware of possible default situations. To determine the sources of delinquencies and defaults, it is vital to consider the borrower, the property, the market, or a combination of the three.

There is no standardized approach to restructuring loans. The complex nature of commercial loans necessitates a creative and tailored approach for each situation. A restructured loan may result in a variety of options such as a cash flow mortgage, a reduced payment rate, forgiveness, or a reduction in the loan amount.

■ Strategies To Detect Defaults

To maintain an acceptable level of delinquencies in the current commercial real estate environment requires a proactive, rather than a reactive, approach. Troubled real estate situations need to be addressed before they become delinquent or reach a point of default. A strategy that allows the loan administrator to continually review the portfolio for early warning signs of a possible default is essential. At a minimum, this strategy should include the following factors:

- Perform physical property inspections
- Review property operating statements
- Review property real estate tax payments
- Review property insurance coverage
- Monitor the timeliness of debt service payments

Physical Property Inspections

The purpose of the property inspection is to monitor the physical and investment quality of the loan and ensure that the property is maintained in accordance with the original underwriting standards. The results of this monitoring activity can serve to provide an early warning device that may signal potential problems regarding the borrower's ability to adequately maintain the property and make monthly debt service payments.

Upon completion of the property inspection, noted deferred maintenance items are referred to the borrower for resolution. Follow-up (possible re-inspection) must be performed to assure deferred maintenance items are cured. Rent rolls should be verified with tenants in place and leases reviewed for authenticity. Properties exhibiting substantial deferred maintenance, tenant vacancies, or non-compliance disputes with the borrower over the correction of these items should be constantly supervised for future problems.

Property Operating Statements

Annual property operating statements should be required on all income-producing properties. The object is to examine and provide commentary on any significant changes in the operations and provide an early warning mechanism on potential problem loan situations. This analysis should be designed to

- explain the reasons for debt coverages less than the original underwriting standards;
- explain the reasons for decline in income or the abnormal increase in operating expenses;
- comment on trends when comparing past period statements; and
- indicate a forecast for the property.

Operating statements that reveal unusual variances from prior years should be investigated until a satisfactory explanation is found, or carefully scrutinized for future problems.

Property Real Estate Taxes

In monitoring the payment of taxes, the obvious solution is to collect a monthly escrow and make payments directly to the taxing authority. In those instances where taxes are not escrowed, evidence from either the borrower or the applicable taxing authorities must be obtained to assure that all obligations are current. Should the borrower fail to provide evidence of payment, or worse, not make the appropriate payments, attempts should be made to immediately establish a repayment plan for the delinquent taxes as well as escrowing for future tax obligations. Resistance by the borrower, claims of inadequate cash flow, or a lack of cooperation could be an early warning signal of a potential problem and should be monitored closely, particularly in the case of nonpayment of taxes, which may precipitate the need to take action to preserve the asset.

Property Insurance

Like taxes, property insurance must be constantly monitored. The borrower and/or insurer should provide evidence of the current property insurance in force. The loan administrator should review for adequate coverage and maintain evidence of this review in the servicing file. Resistance by the borrower to provide insurance information might result in the loan administrator replacing property insurance to provide adequate protection. Nonpayment of premiums or a reduction in coverage may also provide substantial risks for the investor and require constant supervision.

Timely Debt Service Payments

Constant review of delinquency reports revealing familiar names month after month or payment histories showing receipt of payments later and later in the month indicate a borrower with cash flow problems, requiring constant supervision for possible future problems. Nonpayment obviously signals a problem situation and requires immediate action by the loan administrator or investor.

The information provided through early warning signals assists the loan administrator in assessing the situation and determining the extent to which further action is warranted. Troubled real estate situations need to be addressed before they become delinquent or default. Preemptive action allows both the borrower and investor maximum room to maneuver. In the long run, it will reduce costs and cut losses that usually accompany a more adversarial workout. In addition, early action could minimize the time in which the underlying security may deteriorate.

■ Sources of Delinquencies and Defaults

Once the loan administrator has been alerted to a potential problem, it is important to determine not only the magnitude but the underlying cause of the problem. Effective communication between the borrower, loan administrator, and investor is extremely important at this point. All problems need to be addressed aggressively and honestly to determine if the problem is with the borrower, the property, the market, or a combination of all three. Based on this review, the investor will decide if it is feasible to consider a workout and/or a restructuring of the debt.

The process of developing workout and/or disposition strategies should include an analysis of the borrower's capabilities, the property's characteristics, and the market in which it is competing. Failure to consider or accurately assess any one of these factors could lead to less than optimal results and add to an investor's loss exposure.

Borrower Considerations

When analyzing the capabilities of borrowers, consideration must be given to their perception of the problem and whether they are being realistic in their evaluation of the situation. What is the borrower's current role in the property? Does the borrower manage, lease, and/or market the property? Does the borrower possess the necessary skills to provide optimal benefits? Mismanagement and/or absentee ownership are often the root cause for a problem loan. An important question in this analysis is whether the borrower adds value to the property by his or her ownership, or whether the investor would be better secured by the borrower being removed from ownership. The credibility of the borrower is also an important consideration.

Property Issues

In dealing with property issues, many investors will rely solely on the appraisal process to come to a conclusion of value. Unfortunately, appraisals are point-in-time values with varied assumptions. One individual's opinion may not always provide a true current status of the property. Appraisals are only one piece of the puzzle when dealing with property issues. Investors must assess vacancy rate volatility and compare prior period income and expenses to current numbers, noting significant variations, in order to determine what caused the changes.

Other property issues of concern could require a detailed property inspection to determine the structural soundness, code compliance, and environmental issues that surround the property. In addition, one should analyze how the subject property compares and/or competes with other properties of a similar nature within a reasonable market environment. In addition to these economic issues, the investor must consider the accounting and regulatory issues involved in a restructuring.

Market Factors

The market status of the property can be the most difficult issue to assess as well as understand, yet market issues may far outweigh borrower and property concerns and end up being the most important factor in the investor's decision on how to move forward on a problem property. One must become aware of the dynamics of the competing market. Is there an abundance of inventory of competing units? What is the competition doing in relation to pricing and/or rental concessions? What are the long-term prospects for the property? Each of the above-mentioned components must be fully understood in order to formulate an effective strategy for any workout or disposition. This process can also be used as an effective tool to learn from mistakes previously made when considering future lending and workout decisions.

Pre-Workout Options

Upon determining the underlying problem, the investor must evaluate which alternative makes the best economic sense, a workout or foreclosure. The investor must consider the cost of foreclosing and selling the underlying property compared with the cost of restructuring and carrying the loan. For the most part, however, investors are often willing to renegotiate loans with borrowers, so long as their terms are met and they have reasonable assurances that the restructuring plans will work.

Before deciding whether to grant forbearance and/or moratorium, borrowers need be reminded that terms of the mortgage and the right of the investor to take corrective action are not waived even though discussions are taking place that may provide relief for them. The investor and loan administrator may wish to sign a "pre-negotiation" letter with the borrower that sets out the nonbinding terms of such negotiations.

Before entering into any discussions concerning a loan workout with a borrower, many investors require execution of a "pre-workout" letter agreement with the borrower. The general terms and purpose of such an agreement are to require the borrower to acknowledge that any such negotiations do not bind either party nor does the investor waive any of its rights under the loan documents. Such letters are best drafted by the investor's attorney to ensure all local jurisdictional issues are covered.

■ Loan Restructuring Workouts

Advantages and Disadvantages

There is no "ABC" approach to restructuring a loan; each is unique. The complex nature of commercial loans, increased accounting and regulatory scrutiny, and the lack of liquidity in the general market necessitates a sometimes creative and tailored approach for each project.

Basic advantages of restructuring a loan could include the following:

■ Returning the loan to a performing status
■ Keeping the borrower in place as owner of the real estate and using his or her property management and/or marketing expertise to bring the workout to a successful conclusion
■ Creating incentives for the borrower to complete the restructuring as planned
■ Possible investor participation in any future gains in the property's upside
■ Limiting ownership liabilities such as those involving hazardous waste or environmental problems in lieu of the investor taking title to the property
■ Not having to add foreclosed properties to an investor's portfolio with the associated costs and management issues
■ Avoidance of possible bankruptcy protection on behalf of the borrower which may prove costly to the investor

Disadvantages surrounding restructures could include the following:

■ Leaving an untrustworthy borrower in control of the collateral, risking further dissipation of the asset
■ Developing a restructured plan that the borrower cannot possibly accomplish
■ Developing a restructured plan that is complicated and difficult to admin-ister
■ Continued close monitoring of the loan to assure full compliance with the plan
■ Having to report a loan as restructured and carry it as a classified item for at least the duration of the restructured plan

■ Provisions of Loan Restructuring

As previously noted, restructured loans are unique and are customized to meet the needs of both the borrower and investor. A restructured loan may contain one or more of the following provisions:

Payment Moratorium

Under this scenario, a borrower will discontinue making monthly debt service payments for a stated period of time. These discontinued payments can be treated various ways, ranging from total forgiveness to a capitalization of these payments and a reamortization of the loan over the remaining term.

Cash Flow Mortgage

Here the borrower is required to pass on to the investor any remaining cash flow after the property income and expenses have been accounted for. Again, a cash flow mortgage should be for a distinct period of time and the deficient debt service payments can either be forgiven or capitalized and reamortized over the remaining term of the loan.

Adjusting the Interest Rate

Here the investor adjusts the interest rate downward to enable the borrower to make monthly debt service payments. As cash flow of the property improves, this interest rate can be stepped up and will eventually exceed the initial coupon rate. The intent of this type of restructure is that over the period of the loan the average interest rate received will equate to the original coupon rate.

Reduced Payment Rate

If the property is considered good security and is experiencing a temporary interruption of cash flow, a reduction in the amount of the payment could be considered for a period of time. The balance of the unpaid interest would be deferred and either amortized over the remaining term of the loan after the restructure period or a balloon payment at maturity.

Balloon Payment

Occasionally it may be necessary to postpone the collection of any deferred principal and interest payments until the end of the moratorium term or until some future date.

Interest Only

It may be that the property's cash flow cannot substantiate the monthly principal and interest payment. Under the interest only method, for a period of time the investor may collect only interest at the coupon rate, deferring any principal payment to the end of the mortgage term, at which time a balloon payment would be required.

Forgiveness

When granting the moratorium, the investor may decide that interest to be deferred may never be collected. In this instance the investor will forgive the interest obligation, realizing that it can never be paid.

Reduction in Loan Amount

In extreme cases, the investor may agree to reduce the amount of the loan and forgo the amount reduced or convert it to subordinate debt or an equity position in the property.

When restructuring a loan, an investor should determine if the borrower has any additional collateral to offer, possibly in the form of guarantees or other real property, to enhance its position.

Once a restructure with the borrower has been agreed upon, the agreement must be properly documented, including all repayment terms and conditions that are planned to go into effect. The usual method of documenting a restructured loan is to prepare a modification agreement, modifying the terms of the note and deed of trust or mortgage. Investors should also take this opportunity to review their loan documents and negotiate with the borrower any other modifications that may be beneficial to the investor (i.e., closing "loopholes" in the original documents). All documentation should be reviewed by both the borrower's and investor's counsel and executed by both the mortgagor and the mortgagee. The deed of trust or mortgage modification agreement should be recorded if required, and title insurance endorsements may also become necessary. If junior liens are in existence at the time of the restructure, written consent to the restructure and subordination to any additional funding would be required.

Upon execution of the documents, it is the responsibility of both the borrower and investor to live by the terms of the agreement. In addition, the investor may want to closely scrutinize this loan by obtaining monthly operating statements and performing periodic inspections in order to ensure that the terms of the modification are being followed.

Restructurings are typically of limited duration, intended to assist the borrower through a difficult cash flow period. At the end of the negotiated restructure/moratorium term, the investor has the opportunity to reassess the situation and respond accordingly. Options include extending the existing agreement, modifying the restructuring in light of the current situation, or instituting legal action. Hopefully, however, the modification of the original loan documents succeeded in addressing the problem and the borrower is able to meet his or her obligations once again.

■ Summary

This Chapter focused on the commercial property workouts available for loan delinquencies and defaults. Conducting property inspections, reviewing operating statements, tax payments, insurance coverage, and the timeliness of debt service payments provides insight into potential problem loans.

Problem loans are related to borrower characteristics and property and market issues. Borrower mismanagement and/or absentee ownership are often the main causes for loan delinquencies and defaults. In addition to the appraisal, investors must also assess such items as vacancy rate volatility, structural soundness, and environmental issues of the property. Becoming aware of the dynamics of the competing market is the most difficult to assess but the most important factor to consider.

The advantages and disadvantages of loan restructuring workouts were covered as well as the common provisions found in restructured loans. Payment moratorium, adjusting the interest rate, interest only, and forgiveness are just a few of the provisions available. These provisions are designed to meet the varied needs of both the borrower and investor.

■ Chapter 9 Review Questions

1. The factors to consider when developing a strategy to detect potential defaults include all of the following *EXCEPT*

   a. property inspections.

   b. operating statements.

   c. real estate tax payments.

   d. inferred maintenance items.

   e. timeliness of debt service payments.

2. What party is responsible for providing evidence of the current property insurance in force?

   a. Borrower or insurer

   b. Insurer or lender

   c. Insurer or loan administrator

   d. Borrower or loan administrator

3. Check the items that should be analyzed when developing a workout or disposition of strategy.

   _____ Market

   _____ Appraisal

   _____ Investor equity

   _____ Borrower capabilities

   _____ Property characteristics

4. Property issues are often linked to delinquencies and defaults. In the case of determining the value of property, an appraisal is the only procedure to use.

   a. True

   b. False

5. What is *NOT* an advantage of restructuring a loan?

   a. Returns the loan to a performing status

   b. Prohibits borrower from declaring bankruptcy

   c. Limits ownership liabilities in lieu of the investor taking title to the property

   d. Creates incentives for the borrower to complete the planned restructuring

6. A restructured loan must be reported as such and, at least for the duration of the restructured plan, must be carried as a

   a. property lien.

   b. classified item.

   c. collateral risk.

   d. non-performing loan.

7. Match the description with the appropriate restructuring provision.

   _____ Forgiveness

   _____ Balloon payment

   _____ Payment moratorium

   _____ Cash flow mortgage

   a. Under a moratorium, an investor agrees not to collect the deferred interest.

   b. Borrower passes on to investor the remaining cash flow after the property income and expenses have been accounted for.

   c. Borrower discontinues making monthly debt service payments for a specific period of time.

   d. Postpones the collection of deferred principal and interest payments until the end of the moratorium or some future date.

8. Which restructuring provision allows for the collection of interest at the coupon rate and defers principal payments to the end of the mortgage term?

   a. Interest only

   b. Deferred interest

   c. Reduced payment rate

   d. Reduction of principal

Foreclosure

Upon completion of this chapter, you should be able to

- determine the strategies used for loan delinquencies and defaults;

- identify the alternative methods of foreclosure;

- ascertain the primary methods of foreclosure;

- discern the components of a mortgagee in possession;

- identify the steps used in preparing for a foreclosure acquisition;

- distinguish the main components in administering the assets of foreclosure properties; and

- discern the main components in leasing properties.

■ Introduction

Construction investors have been heard to say that the first phase of a "workout" in today's real estate market is actually closing the loan. At least for the near future, workouts and restructurings will continue to be a fact of life in real estate financing.

When workout negotiations reach an impasse or the workout fails, however, investors are forced to pursue their remedies under the loan documents in order to protect their investment. The exercise of these rights and remedies is a complex process, requiring advice from experienced mortgage bankers and real estate/workout attorneys and, in many instances, the services of a title insurance company, a real estate appraiser, an environmental consultant, and a property manager.

This Chapter presents a general overview of the remedy of foreclosure. Particular attention is paid to judicial foreclosure, the most widely used procedure. Related issues such as deeds-in-lieu of foreclosure and investor liability concerns also are discussed. Several topics, such as the assignment of rents and mortgagee-in-possession status, are reviewed in terms of their roles in the foreclosure process.

■ Strategies for Delinquencies and Defaults

It is important for investors and counsel when involved early on to establish goals when confronted with non-performing or underperforming loans. In formulating such goals, it is important to thoroughly analyze the borrower and the surrounding circumstances. The important questions may be the following: Do you want to take title to the property? What is its value? Where is it located? Is there any equity in the property? Is the property raw land, a partially completed residential subdivision, an inner-city high-rise, or a suburban industrial facility? Is it income producing? Are there environmental concerns? Each of these considerations may lead to different goals and desired outcomes. Once an investor has determined what his or her goal is with respect to a particular property, very often the strategy will dictate itself.

Borrower Motivations

It is important to understand the motivations and the needs of the borrower. For instance, an investor would want to know if a borrower is experiencing other financial difficulties. Does the borrower have exposure to other creditors on this project and on other projects? Have trade creditors obtained judgments or filed liens? Is bankruptcy likely for the borrower? Is the borrower an individual, partnership, corporation, or a limited partnership? Is the property the major or only asset of the borrower?

A thorough understanding of a borrower's current financial condition and a sense of a borrower's long-term chances for survival are crucial to any investor. An analysis of the following matters will assist an investor in deciding on a prudent course of action:

- Current net income available to pay interest and principal installments on the debt
- The borrower's financial resources beyond the income produced from the loan collateral
- The market conditions that will influence the future potential of the property
- The management capability of the borrower
- The property's physical condition, with particular emphasis on deferred maintenance and economic and functional obsolescence
- The attitude and degree of cooperation received from the borrower in recognizing that a problem exists and its willingness to resolve it
- The "track record" and reputation of the borrower for successfully restructuring troubled loans
- The borrower's tax motivations with respect to the property

Investors may choose to take an aggressive stance by seizing rents, obtaining judgments against a borrower, or suing guarantors personally, entering into possession as a mortgagee-in-possession or through a receiver. They may choose to start with preliminary workout discussions, always with the goal of forcing a borrower to the desired result.

Of course, each of these options must be analyzed differently depending on the jurisdiction in which each property or borrower is located. For instance, in some jurisdictions an investor's interest under an assignment of rents must be "perfected" by notifying tenants in writing in accordance with the terms of loan documents so as to protect the investor's position, and this must be done before a bankruptcy petition is filed. Otherwise, they are not considered cash collateral and can continue to be used by the bankrupt debtor. Depending on the type of property (e.g., an apartment building or strip shopping center), seizing control of the rents may be crucial. Of course, an investor must understand and anticipate the time that it will take to proceed along any of these avenues, including the likelihood of successfully completing a foreclosure action.

■ Foreclosure Alternatives

Forbearance by investors from exercising their remedies under the loan documents can take many forms. One of the most common is the so-called 30-60 day catch-up schedule, during which time the borrower agrees in writing to bring the loan current by a certain date.

Before entering into any discussions of loan modification, forbearance, or workout, many investors require execution of a "preworkout" letter agreement with the borrower. The general terms and purpose of such an agreement are to require the borrower to acknowledge that any such negotiations do not bind either party nor does the investor waive any rights under the loan documents. Such letters are best drafted by the investor's attorney to be sure all local jurisdictional issues are covered.

Loan Modification

Modifying the terms of the loan to permit any one or a combination of the following forms of relief also may be appropriate:

- Interest only at the contract rate for a fixed period of time
- Reduced interest, with the differential from the contract rate deferred and accrued to maturity of the loan or a certain future date
- Application of property cash flow to debt service
- Moratorium on debt service payments, with all income from the property used to pay real estate taxes
- Reduction in the loan amount and conversion of a portion of the loan to an equity interest in the property

Deed-in-Lieu

A borrower may agree to tender a deed-in-lieu of foreclosure to an investor. In this extrajudicial method of foreclosure, a borrower conveys the property in fee to an investor to satisfy the mortgage obligation. Not all jurisdictions permit this type of debt extinguishment rather than foreclosure. The principal advantage of an investor's acceptance of a deed-in-lieu of foreclosure over a foreclosure action is that it avoids a great deal of the expense, delay, and publicity that frequently accompanies a public foreclosure sale. In addition, a deed-in-lieu of foreclosure often will not be subject to realty transfer tax; both state and local (city or county) laws must be consulted, however, since laws vary. Some states tax the recordation of the deed, while others tax the delivery of the deed. This distinction is important when considering whether to place a deed in escrow during a forbearance period.

Placing a deed-in-lieu in escrow has been held to constitute "delivery" in some jurisdictions. In Pennsylvania, for instance, the current state transfer tax of 1 percent of the "value of the real estate" (based on an assessed value) is not applicable to the "transfer by a mortgagor to the holder of a bona fide mortgage in default in lieu of a foreclosure or a transfer pursuant to a judicial sale in which the successful bidder is the bona fide holder of a mortgage." Similarly, most counties in Pennsylvania do not impose a transfer tax upon the recordation of a deed-in-lieu of foreclosure. Philadelphia, in contrast, currently does not offer a transfer tax exemption for recordation of deeds in lieu of foreclosure or sheriff's deeds. This is not an insignificant point given that the rate of realty transfer tax in Philadelphia is 3.46 percent. Such a tax can determine an investor's decision whether to accept a deed from its borrower. Accepting a deed-in-lieu is not without disadvantages and risks. These include

- securing the cooperation of the borrower,
- merger doctrine concerns,
- a potential bankruptcy filing, and
- junior liens.

First, investors will not be able to take title to the property by deed-in-lieu of foreclosure unless the borrower cooperates. The facts and circumstances of each negotiation will vary, of course, and there is no guarantee that a borrower will be willing to peaceably part with its property. Conversely, a borrower cannot force an investor to accept a deed-in-lieu.

Second, investors hold both the mortgage and the deed relating to the same property. They are confronted with the prospect of the application of doctrine of merger. This doctrine operates to merge the two estates, resulting in the divestment of the mortgage lien. As a result, junior liens may intervene and assume a priority position to an investor's vesting of title. The applicability of the merger doctrine will vary from jurisdiction to jurisdiction. In any event, language should be drafted into the deed-in-lieu of foreclosure to evidence the intention of the parties that both estates survive, including the investor's rights under the mortgage to foreclose out junior liens and encumbrances at a later date. In some jurisdictions the merger will occur as a matter of law, in which case the lien of the mortgage will be divested and the grantee will have taken the property subject to the junior liens.

Third, when a borrower subsequently files for bankruptcy, a deed-in-lieu of foreclosure may be set aside by the bankruptcy court as either: (a) an avoidable preference (if recorded 90 days prior to the bankruptcy filing) or (b) a fraudulent conveyance (if recorded one year prior to the bankruptcy filing). State law on fraudulent conveyances (typically pursuant to the Uniform Fraudulent Conveyance Act) also may come into play.

Finally, the recording of a deed-in-lieu of foreclosure does not discharge junior liens. If a property is free of junior liens (as revealed by a current title report), a deed-in-lieu of foreclosure remains an attractive option. Otherwise, if there are junior judgments and liens on the property, it may be necessary to record the deed-in-lieu of foreclosure and subsequently to foreclose on the investor's interest under the mortgage to wipe out junior liens so as to obtain "free and clear" title.

■ Foreclosure Proceedings

Foreclosure is a proceeding by which an investor (mortgagee), upon default by a borrower (mortgagor), arranges for the property that is encumbered by the mortgage to be sold to satisfy the debt or a portion of the debt depending on the sale price. Foreclosure terminates the mortgagor's equitable right of redemption, if any, subject to any applicable right of redemption period.

Foreclosure proceedings widely differ from jurisdiction to jurisdiction. Some states have relatively straightforward procedures, while others remain complicated and ill-defined. Some states provide for a sheriff's sale of the property, while others require that a court-appointed trustee conduct the sale. Every state permits judicial foreclosure in some form.

State statutes typically require that the sale of a property must be advertised to the general public by a combination of posting of the property and newspaper notices. Other interested parties, including junior mortgagees, judgment creditors, and tenants receive notice of the sale in some other prescribed fashion, typically by ordinary mail in the case of judgment creditors and by registered or certified mail in the case of the owner of the property. In Pennsylvania, for instance, all such parties are required to receive notice of the sale at least 30 days before the sale date.

Special attention should be paid to the "super-notice and service" requirements that a foreclosing party must meet when property is subject to a federal tax lien. (A routine title search should uncover such a lien.) Specifically, the United States should be named as a party in an action to foreclose a mortgage or other lien on the property. Specific requirements relating to notice, service, and pleading must be met before such a lien will be discharged. Nevertheless, the United States may redeem the property for 120 days after sale for tax liens and one year for nontax sales, 28 U.S.C.A. § 2410; 26 U.S.C.A. §7425. In certain instances, the right to redeem may be waived by the United States.

Analyzing the facts and circumstances surrounding a problem loan may reveal that any form of restructuring or forbearance is not in an investor's best interests. Investors should remember that they have no legal duty or obligation to work out the loan or to grant relief in any form. Investors may well determine that their goals with respect to the property will most likely be realized by instituting foreclosure proceedings. The following steps generally are taken by them in order to institute foreclosure proceedings:

- If he or she has not already done so, the investor should engage an experienced real estate/workout attorney in the jurisdiction where the property is located.
- The investor should forward to counsel all relevant loan documentation, along with a letter explaining the nature of the defaults (both monetary and nonmonetary) and copies of any demand or collection letters already sent to the borrower by the investor. Counsel should review thoroughly the loan documentation, order a title search and, if appropriate, a Phase I environmental audit. If a property is used for industrial or manufacturing purposes, a more extensive environmental examination may be necessary.
- The investor then should review with counsel the options available to the investor, including both the advantages and disadvantages of instituting a foreclosure action. The procedures involved in a foreclosure action vary widely from jurisdiction to jurisdiction. Key issues to consider are the time

and expense involved in completing the sale (under both a default judgment and a contested foreclosure scenario), and the likelihood of a bankruptcy filing (both voluntary and involuntary) prior to completion of the foreclosure sale.

Simultaneously with the foregoing, an investor should take the following steps:

- Determine the current fair market value of the property; obtaining a realistic appraisal is imperative.
- Where deferred maintenance, waste, structural deficiencies, or defective mechanical equipment are at issue, engage a competent engineer to determine the costs of curing any problems.
- Review local market conditions and prepare a report of the property's economic potential.

Once the foregoing review has been completed, a decision whether to foreclose on the property, negotiate with the borrower to have it deliver a deed-in-lieu of foreclosure, sell the mortgage at a discount, or abandon the investment should be made.

If the decision is made to institute foreclosure proceedings, the investor's counsel (if it has not already done so) should notify the borrower (and any other parties required to receive such notice under the loan documents, e.g., guarantors) in writing that an event of default has occurred under the loan documents and that the outstanding principal balance of the loan, together with interest accrued thereon and all other sums due and owing, have been accelerated. Notice should be given in accordance with the terms in the loan documents, and all defaults (both monetary and nonmonetary) should be clearly set forth in the notice. Counsel should make sure that all notice and grace or cure periods (if any) have expired before an event of default is declared under the loan documents.

There may be instances where, because of market conditions, no foreseeable prospect of returning the property to economic viability exists. In such a case, an investor, in the absence of an ability to sell the loan at any price, may abandon further collection efforts and simply leave the mortgage in place, clouding the record title. The risk is that a tax sale of the property would extinguish the investor's interest. If an investor's decision to abandon the property is based on environmental concerns, it may choose to satisfy the mortgage to break any ties it may have to the subject property. If a personal guaranty is in place, an investor may consider filing a civil action directly against the guarantors.

■ Main Methods of Foreclosure

The two most widely recognized and commonly used methods of foreclosure are judicial sale foreclosure and power of sale foreclosure. A third, and little used, method of foreclosure is strict foreclosure. Only judicial sale and power of sale foreclosure are discussed below.

Judicial Sale

Foreclosure proceedings vary widely from state to state. Judicial foreclosure is the most widely used foreclosure mechanism. It also can be the most technical, expensive, and time-consuming. In Philadelphia, for instance, it currently is estimated that under ideal circumstances (that is, the borrower/defendant fails to file an answer to the investor's complaint and a default judgment is entered), a foreclosure action by public judicial sale takes approximately four months to complete.

Judicial Sale Procedures   As a general matter, judicial foreclosure entails either joining in the foreclosure proceeding or formally notifying all parties who have an interest in the property to be sold. A title search must be ordered and reviewed in order to identify these parties, which may include the owner of a property (if the fee owner is not the same entity as the borrower/mortgagor), tenants (if leases have been recorded), junior mortgagees, and judgment creditors, among others. Local law will dictate what type of notice is due each of these parties.

A foreclosure action is commenced by filing a complaint in mortgage foreclosure in the county where the land is located. Depending on local procedure, the complaint may be required to recite the amount and facts concerning the debt, including the default giving rise to the investor's right to foreclose the parties to and the date of the mortgage contract, any assignments thereof, the place of record of the mortgage, a description of the property, a specific averment of default, an itemized statement of the amounts due and owing, and a demand or prayer for relief.

Notice of process is then served on the defendant in order to notify him or her of the commencement of the action. The defendant is then afforded a certain period of time within which to file an answer (often 30 days). Possible defenses to the investor's action may include allegations that the borrower/defendant is not in default, that an extension of time was granted by the investor, that the mortgage was satisfied or released, or that improper notice was given.

In Pennsylvania, for example, a judgment in mortgage foreclosure is said to be an *in rem* or *de terris* action, restricted to the mortgaged property. The judgment against the property relates back to the date of the mortgage lien. An *in rem* proceeding differs from an *in personam* proceeding, which results in a judgment against an obligor generally, the satisfaction of which is not restricted to the mortgaged property. If a foreclosure judgment has been obtained, an investor may direct the sheriff, or a trustee, if applicable, to attach the property pursuant to a writ of execution or an order of the court. A judgment on a note pursuant to an *in personam* proceeding, by contrast, can attach to any of a debtor's real or personal property in order to satisfy the judgment; and in such case an investor is not limited to satisfaction out of the mortgaged property.

The proceeds obtained from a foreclosure sale typically are applied first to unpaid taxes (both state and local), then to court costs, and finally to discharge the mortgage obligation. Where the proceeds of the foreclosure sale exceed the mortgage obligation (which is the exception and not the rule), the balance is paid to the mortgagor so long as there are no other liens or encumbrances against the property. If there are junior mortgages or judgment creditors, the excess funds are distributed to them in accordance with the priority of their respective claims, which in many states is set by statute.

In Pennsylvania, the Rules of Civil Procedure provide that within 30 days of the sale of real property, the sheriff must prepare and file for inspection a schedule of proposed distribution of the sale proceeds. If written exceptions to the proposed distribution schedule are not received within 10 days after the filing, the proceeds shall be distributed in accordance with the sheriff's schedule. No such schedule of distribution is required when the property is "sold" to the foreclosing party.

As a general matter, judicial foreclosure sales are scheduled on a regular basis, often monthly, by an officer of the court, typically the sheriff. The sales usually are held "on the courthouse steps." Quite often, there is no third-party bidding at the sale and the property simply is sold to the foreclosing party "for a dollar plus costs of suit." A lack of competitive bidding does not create a problem. Indeed, competitive bidding is more the exception than the rule when dealing with commercial properties. So long as the sale is advertised properly, open to the public, and conducted fairly, it is immaterial whether third-party bids are made at a sale. In short, proper notice of the sale to the defendant and other interested parties in accordance with the applicable local rules should be the primary concern of the investor's counsel.

After the sale is complete, the court may, depending on the jurisdiction, confirm the sale. Not all states require court confirmation. If there is no period of redemption, the sheriff's deed passes title to the purchaser.

Bidding Factors at Judicial Sales   Notwithstanding the fact that competitive bidding is the exception and not the rule at judicial sales of real property, an investor or its representative nonetheless must be prepared with a maximum bid at the sale. Factors to consider when formulating a maximum bid include

- the judgment amount,
- court costs,
- prior liens,
- the trustee's or sheriff's commission,
- realty transfer taxes, and
- the fair market value of the property.

If there is competitive bidding at the sale and if an investor has determined that the fair market value of the property is greater than the debt owed plus applicable costs and expenses, then an investor's maximum bid should equal the amount of the debt plus costs and expenses, assuming such an amount constitutes "reasonably equivalent value" (as more fully discussed below).

If the fair market value of the property is determined by an investor to be less than the amount of the debt plus costs and expenses, and assuming that there is no possibility under the applicable state law for a deficiency judgment recovery, the investor might consider "cutting its losses" by allowing a third-party bidder to be the successful bidder for an amount equal to fair market value plus costs and expenses. Of course, all of this assumes that the foreclosing party is the first mortgagee. Bidding strategies become considerably more complicated when a junior mortgagee or judgment creditor is the foreclosing party.

As suggested, the successful bidder at a judicial sale also must be wary of paying a "reasonably equivalent value" for the property. This concern was raised by the case of *Durrett v. Washington National Insurance Co.,* 621 F.2d 201 (5th Cir. 1980) and has received considerable attention elsewhere. Note, however, that *Durrett* involved a residential foreclosure, that the borrower/defendant was found to have considerable equity in the property, and that some courts outside the Fifth Circuit have declined to adopt the *Durrett* approach to "reasonably equivalent value."

A final comment on deficiencies is appropriate. Where a sale brings less than the amount owed on the indebtedness, a deficiency exists; local law will determine whether an investor has a right to collect a deficiency. In Pennsylvania, for instance, the law provides that there is no right to a deficiency in an *in rem* (i.e., mortgage foreclosure) action; such a right only exists in an *in personam* (i.e., civil action or confessed judgment on the note) action. Many mortgages contain an exculpatory clause whereby a borrower will not be held personally liable for the debt. In such instances, an investor will have to look solely to the mortgage security if a foreclosure sale occurs, thus barring any right to pursue a deficiency claim.

Power of Sale Foreclosure

Foreclosure by power of sale is an alternative method of foreclosure. Under this foreclosure device, an investor or a trustee sells the property upon default by a borrower pursuant to a clause in the mortgage or the deed of trust. Under the terms of a deed of trust, the trustee holds the security "in trust" for an investor, and the principal function of the trustee is to conduct a foreclosure sale of the property upon default.

Power of sale foreclosure, which is not judicially supervised, generally is recognized as less procedurally cumbersome and less expensive than judicial sale foreclosure. Notice requirements, for example, are much less exacting under power of sale foreclosure than judicial foreclosure, particularly with respect to notifying junior lien holders of the scheduled sale.

It is often said that a purchaser at a nonjudicial foreclosure sale buys the property at its peril; accordingly, it is most advisable for a purchaser to first examine the chain of title for possible defects before the sale. A successful bidder receives a deed or certificate of sale describing the property, stating the purchase price as well as the costs and fees of sale.

Finally, it is important to keep in mind that a mortgagee, while vested with a power of sale in the mortgage or deed of trust, has the option of proceeding with a judicial sale if it so elects. It is also the case that unless statutorily authorized, there is no right of redemption following foreclosure by power of sale.

■ Foreclosure-Related Method

Mortgagee in Possession

Although jurisdictions differ and local law must be consulted in each case, the broad view seems to be that investors will not be considered mortgagees in possession if they merely receive rents from borrowers or their agents on account of the mortgaged debt. However, active efforts on the part of investors to collect the rents may create the status of a mortgagee in possession. A mortgagee who seizes the rents does not become the owner of the mortgaged property, but rather a "quasi or constructive trustee" for the owner, to whom he or she must account for the rent seized and for the proper management of the property.

Therefore, a mortgagee in possession would be wise in applying the rents in the following order of priority: taxes, insurance, repairs and maintenance, interest and principal on the mortgage. Also, a mortgagee's operation of the property must be in accordance with a "prudent owner" standard. This entails a duty to make sure that the property continues to be productive. As always, the applicable state law in this area should be consulted before an investor considers taking control of a property.

Indeed, on balance, an investor does not want to be considered a mortgagee in possession unless it is absolutely necessary because such status confers on an investor all of the liabilities an owner of the property would have (e.g., maintenance of the property, lessor and environmental liabilities). However, some of these liabilities may be reduced by provisions of a mortgage or an assignment of rents and leases that provides for an indemnity from the borrower to the investor for any losses resulting from the investor's status as a mortgagee in possession. (Query whether an indemnity has value—often a mortgagee perfects rents when a borrower already is financially troubled.)

Appointment of Receiver   In certain instances following default, a court may appoint a receiver to manage the mortgaged property pending the mortgage foreclosure action. It generally is recognized that a receiver is a fiduciary of the court, appointed to preserve the property and receive its rents, issues, and profits, and to pay out any necessary expenses pending litigation. Determining whether to appoint a receiver rests within the discretion of the court. The requirements for the appointment of a receiver are somewhat similar to those for injunctive relief. Thus, a receiver will not be appointed unless it appears that the appointment is necessary to save the property from injury or threatened loss or dissipation.

Though the requirements for appointment of a receiver are considerable, case law generally recognizes the need for flexibility in the application of these principles to achieve what is equitable and just. It must be emphasized that appointment of a receiver is an equitable remedy which will not be granted except on equitable grounds and for substantial reasons.

One such reason is for the protection of the property. To obtain a receiver, an applicant must demonstrate clearly that the property is in danger of waste or material injury. However, the appointment of a receiver may not be justifiable where it appears that the income of the property already is being applied to the payment of taxes and interest and a partial reduction of the mortgage debt, or when a mortgagee already is in possession of the property, collecting the rents, and providing for the management of the property.

Some jurisdictions such as Florida have quasi-receivership statues that allow for payment of rents into the registry of the court where they can be paid out for protection of the property.

Foreclosure Considerations

Assignment of Rents and Leases

Assignment of rents and leases is a primary concern in any foreclosure action. Moreover, jurisdictions differ over what constitutes "perfection" of an assignment of rents. Accordingly, local laws must be consulted. This topic is addressed more fully elsewhere in this book.

Environmental Liability Concerns

Investors have become increasingly sensitive to environmental liability concerns not only in making the loan but also whenever considering taking a deed-in-lieu of foreclosure, instituting a foreclosure action, or taking over the operations of a property.

Americans with Disabilities Act

The recently enacted Americans with Disabilities Act of 1990 is a sweeping piece of legislation. Although its full impact on commercial financing and foreclosure is not yet clear, it is an area that will receive considerable attention in the near future.

■ Foreclosure Acquisitions

Properties acquired through foreclosure have historically been considered "distressed properties." However, this is misleading because foreclosure acquisitions of real estate owned (REOs) encompass a broad array of properties acquired by mortgagees as a by-product of their lending activities. While a mortgage loan may be underperforming, the underlying security can range from abandoned and vacant to fully leased and occupied. Similarly, the factors leading to investor acquisition can include project economics, general economic conditions, market conditions, excessive debt, ownership problems, and tax law changes.

It's important to treat REOs like any purposeful real estate acquisition, realizing that each project has unique attributes and problems. While there are some considerations unique to REOs, there are few, if any, absolute rules. How each project is handled will depend on the dynamic interplay of the acquiring investor's organization style, philosophy, and financial capability, combined with the individual needs and characteristics of the project.

While an investor may acquire sole ownership of income producing property as the result of a default by a partner in a joint venture, investors are more commonly faced with acquisition of income properties by foreclosure sale or acceptance of a deed-in-lieu of foreclosure from an unaffiliated entity. If investors have had an equity position prior to their acquiring complete ownership of the property, they should be familiar with the financial operation and current and anticipated needs of the property and be able to decide quickly what changes, if any, will be required.

Preparing for Acquisition

It's essential for the investor to begin preparing for a potential foreclosure acquisition well in advance of the anticipated acquisition date. While direct involvement in day-to-day property operations will likely be precluded, the investor should begin thinking like a property owner and should coordinate the efforts of its transfer team to ensure a smooth transition from loan to equity portfolio. The transition team can be a formal or informal group of identified in-house and contract professionals that may include a loan administrator, engineer, and attorney. A coordinated effort is critical if the investor's pre-foreclosure plans are to survive the transition to ownership and be carried out smoothly by the post-foreclosure team. In occupied properties, a coordinated effort imparts a degree of stability in what is otherwise likely to be a tumultuous period for the project and its occupants.

Planning for the possibility of a foreclosure acquisition should begin during the underwriting of every mortgage loan. Adherence to closing requirements, solid loan documentation, and effective post-closing servicing position the investor to effectively identify and handle underperforming assets and prepare for acquisition if necessary. Enforcement of a relatively standard requirement, such as a provision requiring audited financial statements, can aid in the investor's collection of rent escalations in an office building. Failure to refile UCC continuation statements can have drastic consequences for a hospitality operation. If servicing procedures outlined in previous chapters of this text are followed, unnecessary problems can be avoided.

Problem Identification and Approach

Once a problem has been identified, investors need to consider their approach to the situation on an asset-by-asset basis. In the event of default, prior to commencing collection action, the investor should consider under what circumstances it would be willing to acquire title to the security, and under what circumstances it may not be willing to do so. This decision should guide the investor through any foreclosure/bankruptcy proceedings prior to acquisition. While the preliminary decision may be subject to change over time, it focuses the investor on both positive and negative attributes of an asset. The nature of the legal proceedings leading to acquisition, whether a receiver will be appointed, whether a redemption period will apply, etc., will all influence the decision process.

While the ultimate goal of an investor acquiring an REO, either short or long term, is its disposition, the reality is that once acquired, most REOs cannot, regardless of pricing, be immediately disposed of by the acquiring investor. Consequently, the investor should develop both short term and long term plans, and interim contingency plans, for each REO.

Directing and Scheduling Foreclosures

If acquisition is deemed to be a likely outcome, barring the ability to work out a better solution, expedience in gaining control of a project is generally desirable. Delay and uncertainty may do untold physical and psychological harm to a property. The investor should therefore exert whatever control is possible and legally available during the foreclosure/bankruptcy process to ensure that the owner or receiver take reasonable actions through the date of transfer. Various jurisdictions will have unique practices associated with the foreclosure process, some of which, such as sheriff's fees, are negotiable. The investor should identify and take advantage of any such practices.

Some jurisdictions provide little or no real opportunity to affect the scheduling of a foreclosure sale date. Others are more flexible. Deed-in-lieu transfer dates are by their nature negotiable. The timing of a foreclosure acquisition should be closely coordinated between the loan administrator, investor, and legal counsel. Left to chance, the worst possible foreclosure date would likely be assigned (late afternoon on a Friday, a holiday weekend, the first of the month). Since it's not uncommon for an owner in foreclosure, given the opportunity, to attempt to collect rents in advance by legal means or otherwise, strategic foreclosure scheduling can have meaningful impact on the investor's rent collection ability and tenant retention.

Method/Form of Acquisition

The method of acquisition, judicial or nonjudicial foreclosure sale, "friendly" foreclosure, deed-in-lieu or other will depend on many factors including potential liability concerns, the existence of other encumbrances, the relationship between the investor and mortgagor, tenant retention considerations, and transfer taxes (which may differ substantially for foreclosure sale and deed-in-lieu transfers). Whether to hold an REO property in the parent's name or that of a stand-alone entity is also a consideration, based in part on corporate philosophy, property type, and liability considerations.

Budgeting and Portfolio Management

Projected cash flow (positive or negative) and anticipated capital needs should be identified and provided for in your REO portfolio budget for the period in which acquisition is contemplated. Necessary funding sources can then be identified by the investor and will hopefully be available upon transfer. From a portfolio standpoint, other REOs may then be in a position to rely on income from an anticipated acquisition to fund their needs. Failure to adequately budget may render an investor's post-acquisition plans moot for a time.

Acquisition/Transfer to REO Portfolio

Upon acquisition, a team should be prepared with duties such as closing out a receivership, if one existed, payment of real estate and transfer taxes, filing a real estate tax appeal, insuring the REO, securing it (changing locks, winterizing), and inventorying property, all clearly assigned, in order to conclude the transfer and commence management and marketing of the REO.

Operations Analysis

When investors prepare for ownership of an income property, they need to analyze the existing operation, compare it to experience (personal and published), and make projections about future operations through consideration of the current financial statements (balance sheet, operating statement, income/expense statement) to determine the operation's financial viability. The mortgagee will need to determine the most appropriate means for controlling expenses, maintaining or improving revenue, achieving profit (or minimizing loss), and enhancing asset value. Achievement of desired goals may require changes in operating procedures.

The financial strength of the operation, economic conditions, market conditions, and the physical quality of the owned asset are important factors in understanding the valuation of the property and the decision to retain ownership or sell. Failure to understand the current situation will lead to long term problems.

Market Analysis and Property Valuation   A careful review and understanding of the project's market is essential. Available space in competing projects ("competition") must be identified. Market occupancy/vacancy ("utilization") must be studied. Market rental rates and typical tenant improvement allowances must be determined. Absorption rates and trends need to be defined. Most importantly, a property survey should be prepared so a realistic assessment of the REO, in terms of quality, class, attributes, and amenities, can be made.

While a formal fee appraisal, likely obtained during the foreclosure/bankruptcy process, is valuable, it is limited in its usefulness, as there are marked differences between, for example, market value and liquidation value. Due to its formal nature and constraints, an appraisal cannot address all aspects of value as they pertain to the investor's situation. Other value concepts, such as investment value, insurable value, book value, intrinsic value to owner, value in use, liquidation value, loan value, assessed value, sheriff's value, and transfer value also need consideration.

While appraisers may identify value, investors and their representatives need to understand the process to protect the investor's interests. The investor needs to consider the various concepts of value previously noted, and to perform a feasibility analysis, in order to utilize any available valuations for planning or decision purposes. The transfer value will establish the REO's book value, lead to a loss (or gain) on acquisition, and affect the investor's plans to hold, rehabilitate, or sell the asset. To simply accept an appraised value and rely on it for planning purposes is somewhat fruitless if it incorporates a scenario the investor can't accept, is based on a holding period that doesn't match the investor's needs, presumes the undertaking of a rehabilitation program the investor does not agree with, or generally fails to reflect the investor's philosophy. A fee appraisal secured for litigation purposes may simply be inappropriate for ownership decision-making purposes. As with operations analysis, market analysis and valuation are important tools to be utilized by the investor in planning and budgeting.

Due Diligence

The investors should satisfy, as fully as possible (given access restrictions and information limitations) their due diligence requirements. These would include but not be limited to the following:

- A building conditions survey (physical property inspection)
- Environmental inspections
- Site survey
- Code compliance review
- Title review (other liens, easements, leases)
- Tax searches (real estate, sales, income)
- UCC search
- Lease analysis

Delinquent real estate taxes, a common finding, may be payable in order to secure a transfer deed.

The acquiring investor shouldn't, however, pay more than the minimum necessary to obtain the deed while retaining, if available, tax appeal rights. The investor may even be able to arrange to continue a tax appeal initiated prior to transfer. For hospitality properties, which are in effect businesses tied to a specific piece of realty, retention, transfer, or securement of a liquor license or franchise ("flag") may be critical to the ongoing operation. Business licenses and franchise agreements may be critical to the continuation of various other ongoing operations.

Environmental and Code Considerations   For property having environmental concerns stemming from acts or uses that predated the investor's acquisition and possibly even original funding of the loan, the investor will presumably identify and study these aspects prior to acquisition and determine whether they are so onerous as to preclude entering the chain of ownership. Whether resulting from acts of the prior owner or not, any problems, whether or not a violation, will have to be dealt with (not necessarily cured) in order to make the property marketable.

Some environmental concerns such as asbestos containing material (ACM) present somewhat less of a threat today than several years ago. Consequently, if the extent of an environmental problem does not preclude an investor from foreclosing, its mere existence is not likely to require curing the ill. In many cases, an operations and management (O&M) program can effectively address the concern and comply with governmental requirements. Containment, encapsulation, and/or O&M programs in many instances pose a safer approach than does wholesale abatement of ACMs.

This does not imply that abatement is never the appropriate route. Professional consultants should be engaged to determine the extent of any problems and to make appropriate recommendations for correction prior to acquisition. Anticipated costs should be reviewed carefully and steps must be taken to prevent any further violation as quickly as possible.

Environmental concerns may impact on the ability to undertake rehabilitation or demolition. Similarly, other code violations may influence the investor's ability to renovate without triggering code compliance requirements. Grandfathered nonconforming uses, parking requirements, and governmental regulations such as the Americans with Disabilities Act (ADA) also need to be considered when rehabilitation is a consideration.

Potential Liability   Liability concerns, whether they are based on physical, environmental, or other matters, will affect the decision to take title and may dictate the entity type that title will be held in.

Rehabilitation   Whether a sell or hold route is your choice or preference, the investor must still determine whether the property requires refurbishing to make it attractive for marketing (for sale or lease). A factor to be considered is how long the property is realistically expected to be retained. If the investor plans to retain the property for a time or do any rehabilitative work, he or she will want to spend some time and money (even if a limited amount) doing physical work readily visible to tenants and the general public, which, while not addressing the most important physical need(s) of the project, can address an important psychological need of the project (showing that after transfer a positive change is taking place). Many REO names are changed to produce a similar effect and create some distance from the pre-foreclosure product. The existence of a post-foreclosure redemption period will also affect the decision to rehabilitate.

■ Management, Leasing, and Disposition

It is important to match the property management firm, as well as leasing and/or disposition agent(s), with the investor and with each other. Corporate philosophy will be a factor, with many investors unwilling to retain any of the former owner's agents or on-site personnel (except under specific or unusual circumstances where situational characteristics dictate a departure from standard operating procedures). The process of selecting and contracting for management, leasing, and/or disposition agent(s) should be settled well in advance of the acquisition date and be part of a well-planned and coordinated loan administration program.

Management

Investors will need a manager or management firm (property manager) experienced in handling the type of day-to-day operation associated with the REO and will need to determine whether they will employ the services of a fee manager or attempt to operate the REO themselves. Investors who focus on property size, proximity, staffing, and perceived expertise may elect to manage themselves. More commonly, investors will contract for the services of a fee manager or management firm.

In selecting a manager, investors should rely on their personal experience with the property manager, conflicts with competing assignments, possible synergies with other assignments, familiarity of the property manager with the investors and their requirements, the property manager's ability to meet the needs of the investor, and the assignment. The investor may use a known entity, or may want to foster some competition as a basis for comparison. While there should be no conflict of interest among a property manager's various assignments, the existence of competitive assignment may or may not present a conflict. In fact, synergy may result in cost reductions and expense sharing.

The investor's hold/sell position will affect decisions regarding operations, property improvements, and management. A contemplated quick sale may lead ownership to defer recommended improvements or management changes and attempt to simply maintain the building in as attractive a position as possible until a market of potential buyers can be developed. The investor's position on refurbishing and the need to improve the property's financial position needs to be accepted by the property manager. To the investor, the REO may unfortunately be one in a portfolio of many, all vying for an allocation of scarce resources. The investor's perspective may well differ from that of the property manager, which will be property specific. The property manager must be able to work within the investor's framework rather than fight it.

The Management Contract   Whether relying on an investor's or property manager's form, the management contract needs to be reviewed and modified as required for the assignment. Contracts should list the rights and duties of both property manager and owner, the property manager's compensation basis, mutual termination rights and requirements, duration of the assignment, requirements for obtaining fidelity bond and other insurance, the use of third party contract services, budget responsibilities (preparation and limitations on nonbudgeted expenditures), and should specify the property manager's role in marketing the property.

Compensation   A fair compensation package should motivate the property manager and lead to better performance. While investors shouldn't overpay, they should provide an incentive to do good work, particularly with regard to ancillary services and recognizing that the property manager will be gearing up for an assignment that the investor hopes will be short term in nature.

The typical management contract provides for the property manager to receive a periodic fee (typically paid monthly) based on a percentage of gross collected income, a flat fee (appropriate in REO situations where gross income is minimal or erratic), or a combination of both. Incentive fees, particularly in hotel/motel situations, based on the achievement of specified financial goals, may be appropriate. A percentage of sale proceeds upon disposition, within certain preset parameters, may also be appropriate in turn-around situations.

Other Compensation Issues   Property managers may also be allowed to act in a sales brokerage or leasing capacity which would entitle them to compensation for successfully performing such services. A fair compensation structure should eliminate potential conflicts between a property manager's roles as manager, leasing agent, and broker. For direct sales by the investor, the on-site property management staff should, by contract, be expected to show the property on behalf of the investor as a standard service. Because substantial rehabilitation or tenant improvements may be required for an REO, the property manager and owner need to clarify the manager's role and additional compensation, if any, for overseeing construction.

Staffing/Personnel   Distinct from the property management fee paid to the management firm are the salaries paid to the individual manager, assistant manager, and other site staff, which are collectively considered an operating expense payroll. Many REO properties are large enough to require the services of individuals in addition to the manager. Preferably, these individuals should be employees of the property manager. The investor will generally not interact directly with these employees, conducting business through the property manager. Employee benefits as well as benefits customary to a particular operation must be provided and all required employment practices followed. Rather than employing a large staff, a property manager may contract services such as landscaping, janitorial, and elevator maintenance from third parties. All such contracts should be cancelable on 30 days notice or upon sale.

Accounting/Management Reporting   The investor should require operating information on a periodic basis (typically not less than monthly) showing all activity related to the REO's operation. The following should be maintained and provided on a periodic basis (daily, weekly, monthly, annually) as required by the investor:

- Cash reports
- Operating and capital budgets
- Budget variance reports (analyzing actual versus budget)
- On-site accounting records
- Appropriate bank accounts in the name of the owner for security deposits and property operations
- Narrative management reports
- Reconciled bank statements
- Periodic management summaries
- Rent rolls
- Cash and collections reports
- Accounts receivables aging reports
- Delinquent rent aging reports
- Traffic reports
- Move in/move out reports
- Leasing status reports

The degree of detail required in reporting will depend on the operation and the investor's needs. A sample reporting package and required time frames for receipt of property data should all be reviewed with the proposed property manager prior to the engagement. Investors' requirements for use of their own chart of accounts, accounting system, cash versus accrual basis (for various aspects of the operation), data transmission (hard copy, electronically, diskette), periodic clearing or sweeping of accounts, and use of a remittance lock box all need to be discussed to ensure the selection of a compatible property manager.

Depending on the scope of the operation, it may be necessary to have operating statements, budgets, and other reports show income and expenses by operating unit. In the case of a hotel, for example, the statement should be prepared by department (room, restaurant, catering), form being determined by need, with the purpose of alerting the investor of problem areas within the asset's operation.

The prospective manager must consider these aspects in making a proposal. The investor need remember that, when soliciting an account, every management firm believes and will try to convince the investor that it can do the job. The investor needs to see through the sales pitch, review experience, check background, references, financial capacity, and deployment of human resources, determine apparent personality conflicts, philosophical differences, and conflicts of interest.

The selection process should identify the needs of the asset, the requirements of the investor, and the ability of the management firm to fulfill the requirements. While a management contract is not forever, a contract termination will invariably result in some disruption of property operations during transition. Try to do it right the first time. Be willing to make a change if appropriate.

Leasing

Three key areas where the investor will need to focus its attention are commonly classified as management, leasing, and disposition, inseparable parts of the asset administration process.

The investor's approach to leasing will vary depending on property type and size, market conditions, and competitive pressures. For multifamily projects, the property manager will generally handle leasing duties. For office properties, leasing agents not affiliated with the property management firm are not uncommon. The approach should be dictated by the identified needs of the asset, requirements of the investor, and ability of the leasing agent to fill the role. Larger projects may require an on-site staff. Competing assignments need to be considered. A nearby competitive project assignment should not necessarily eliminate a leasing agent from consideration if attributes of the competing project differ somewhat from the investor's project. The investor's project may actually benefit from the competition. The leasing agent, if different from the property manager, will need to coordinate efforts with the manager. The investor must clearly delineate the duties and responsibilities of each.

The Leasing Program   A property specific leasing program must be defined. While a property may need to be maintained or improved to a degree to make it attractive to tenants, capital improvements desired by prospective/existing tenants, and tenant improvements, must be economically justifiable and serve a value enhancing purpose. The purpose may be as direct as adding value to an asset via increased lease income, or indirect via the reduction of carrying costs on a project that should, but cannot be, shut down. The investor may be able to negotiate a position which allows dealing with existing or prospective tenants prior to acquisition. There is an erroneous perception that leasing for the sake of leasing is good. For a given property no leasing may be better than continued leasing. A lease buy-out program aimed at shutting down a project and minimizing losses may be the investor's best alternative.

Capital improvement and tenant improvement costs may be funded by income generated by the asset, or require funding from the investor. Potentially faced with a number of REOs, the investor may have insufficient funds to devote to the project from other sources. In fact, even funds generated by the project may be needed by investors to support other REOs in their portfolio.

Generally, brokers and space users try to avoid "foreclosed properties" for a period of time, so the investor often battles a poor image developed over a relatively long period of time. A viable program based on pre-foreclosure market studies and a realistic assessment of positive and negative attributes of the property and clear identification of the competition is essential. Remarketing, possible repositioning (name change, up or downgrade in class), and reintroduction of the asset to the marketplace (model suites, broker open house) are helpful ways to move REOs.

Standard Forms Standard forms need to be available immediately upon investor acquisition, including a letter of intent, short form and long form lease, work letter, and NDAA (if a prior lien remains in place).

Compensation The investor must establish a fair program that provides reasonable compensation for all aspects of the leasing agent's services, providing an incentive to do a good job, locating quality tenants, and delivering closable transactions that fit the investor's leasing program criteria. Typically, commissions are based on a percentage of lease value, paid over time or discounted, and paid up front, with appropriate rates applicable to new leases, renewals, existing lease options, and co-brokering situations.

Leasing Agent Selection In the process of selecting a leasing agent, the investor considers the building, the needs of the situation, and the ability of a leasing agent to fill the role.

Disposition

The investor may desire a large, small, or virtually no direct role in marketing an asset for sale. The investor will, however, in some capacity, coordinate the disposition process, maintaining a list of available REOs and a contact list of brokers and principals along with their areas of interest (property type, size, location). A marketing package including physical description, lease summaries, current rent roll, lease expiration schedule, and current/historic operating data should be immediately available.

The investor must decide whether to use an open listing, exclusive listing, or even the auction sale route. A nonexclusive listing promotes broad sales interest. An exclusive listing provides more control and minimizes the perception that the property is continually on the market. The investor needs to determine the best approach for each REO.

Standard Forms Standard form documents (listing agreement, letter of intent, sales contract/commitment, form purchase money loan documents, deed, bill of sale) should be available as soon as title passes to the investor to enable the investor to react swiftly to purchase offers.

Generally, investors prefer to sell REOs on an all cash basis but may find it necessary to provide purchase money financing. Typically, an all cash transaction will command a price lower than that which could be obtained if financing were provided. An asset's cash price should reflect the investor's portfolio needs, reinvestment analysis, and property attributes, any of which may make disposition, even at a book loss, a desirable alternative. When financing is required, the purchaser should be required to make a meaningful equity investment to encourage commitment to the property. Equity may be in the form of cash at closing, or funds escrowed for property rehabilitation.

Careful attention should be given to qualifying a purchaser prior to entering into a sales contract, whether or not financing is to be provided. Financial statements and bank references should confirm sufficient liquidity to close the transaction, handle potential operating deficits, and undertake capital improvements. The buyer's background, experience in ownership and management of like kind property, and the experience of any fee manager the purchaser may plan to employ should be investigated.

The Broker's Role and Compensation   Broker registration of clients is of questionable value as unscrupulous brokers will attempt to register a plethora of principals (some of which they've never worked with). Quality professional real estate brokers are an asset in the disposition process. Brokers need to be comfortable with the investor, know they will receive fair compensation for their efforts, and will be dealt with fairly. With a dialogue established and what appears to be a workable offer on the table, the investor will usually deal directly with the proposed purchaser without the broker as intermediary.

Again, while the property is being marketed, it must be maintained. Individual investors have their own opinions about, and approaches to, the disposition process. Pricing should not be inflexible but reflective of market realities, ongoing operations, physical improvements/deterioration, and investor portfolio needs.

Foreclosure Day

The investor's acquisition team is prepared for the expected as well as the unexpected, and will have a property manager on-site as soon as local practice allows, serving appropriate notices to tenants, collecting rents, and securing the premises, as necessary.

■ Summary

This Chapter discussed the strategies used for dealing with loan delinquencies and defaults. It is critical for investors to establish goals when handling nonperforming or underperforming loans. The goals need to be based on borrower motivations, investor preference, and property factors.

Before opting for foreclosure, investors look to alternative methods to deal with problem loans. Loan modification and deeds-in-lieu are common methods used to prevent foreclosure. Loan modification is dependent on the terms and type of loan. A deed-in-lieu is an extrajudicial method of foreclosure where a borrower conveys the property in fee to an investor.

The primary methods of foreclosure are judicial and power of sale. Judicial foreclosures are handled as civil lawsuits and conducted under the auspices of the court. Power of sale foreclosures empower trustees, without court order, to sell property in the event of default and to apply the proceeds to satisfy the obligation, costs, and expenses incurred in the process.

A related foreclosure method is mortgagee in possession. In this case, the lender, due to mortgage default, obtains possession but not ownership of a property. In some instances, a court may appoint a receiver to manage the mortgage property pending foreclosure action.

When preparing for foreclosure acquisitions, it is important to identify problems, direct and schedule events, ensure an acceptable operations analysis, and make sure due diligence reviews are performed. A coordinated effort will help to make the investor's transition to ownership smooth and efficient.

When preparing for the acquisition of foreclosure properties, the management, leasing, and disposition of the properties are crucial parts of the asset administration process. The process of selecting and contracting for management, leasing, and disposition agents should be settled way in advance of the acquisition date and be part of a detailed administrative program.

■ Chapter 10 Review Questions

1. Which is *NOT* an option an investor may take in delinquency or default situations?

   a. Seize rents

   b. Garnish wages

   c. Sue guarantors

   d. Obtain judgment against borrower

2. In delinquency or default situations, an investor will consider the property's physical condition with particular emphasis on incurred maintenance and functional obsolescence.

   a. True

   b. False

3. Which type of agreement often precedes a discussion of loan modification?

   a. Preworkout

   b. Amended terms

   c. Circumstantial deference

   d. Preliminary forbearance

4. All of the following are disadvantages of a deed-in-lieu *EXCEPT*

   a. junior liens.

   b. borrower cooperation.

   c. merger doctrine concerns.

   d. assessment of realty transfer tax.

5. Which method of foreclosure is generally the most technical, expensive, and time-consuming?

   a. Strict

   b. Power of sale

   c. Judicial sale

   d. Circumstantial

6. Unless statutorily authorized, in a power of sale foreclosure, there is no right of

   a. workout.

   b. redemption.

   c. enforcement.

   d. free and clear title.

7. Which term describes a lender, who due to a default, has obtained possession but not ownership of a property?

   a. Lender in title

   b. Mortgagee in trust

   c. Lender in acquisition

   d. Mortgagee in possession

8. After rents are received by a mortgagee in possession, indicate the recommended order of applying the funds from highest (1) to lowest (4).

   _____ Taxes

   _____ Insurance

   _____ Repairs and maintenance

   _____ Principal and interest

9. Check the five areas of consideration when preparing for foreclosure acquisition.

_____ Due diligence review

_____ Loan process analysis

_____ Operations analysis

_____ Method of acquisition

_____ Contamination review

_____ Problem identification and approach

_____ Directing and scheduling foreclosures

10. In addition to the appraised value of property, all of the following values need to be considered in foreclosure acquisitions *EXCEPT*

    a. book.

    b. transfer.

    c. sheriff's.

    d. extrinsic.

    e. liquidation.

11. Leased multifamily projects are generally managed by the

    a. landlord.

    b. leasing agent.

    c. leasing broker.

    d. property manager.

12. Compensation for the staff of leased properties is commonly based on

    a. salary.

    b. salary plus commission.

    c. percentage of lease value.

    d. percentage of occupancy rate.

13. Which is *NOT* a critical component of the asset administration process in foreclosure acquisitions?

    a. Leasing

    b. Disposition

    c. Management

    d. Consolidation

14. An investor can choose to dispose of a property using an open or exclusive listing arrangement or by

    a. renting the property.

    b. auctioning the property.

    c. retaining the property for tax loss purposes.

    d providing attractive refinancing terms for the borrower.

Commercial Mortgage-Backed Securities

learning objectives

Upon completion of this chapter, you should be able to

- identify the role of the servicer in commercial mortgage-backed securities;

- distinguish the common forms of servicing bifurcations;

- recognize the information requirements and restrictions of commercial mortgage-backed securities;

- ascertain the approval programs for commercial mortgage-backed securities servicers; and

- identify the parameters for the transfer or sale of commercial mortgage-backed securities.

Introduction

The securitization of commercial mortgage-backed securities (CMBSs) and the subsequent emergence of a secondary market for them have dramatically changed the role of the commercial servicer. The mortgage banking industry has embraced the term "master servicer" to denote the entity ultimately responsible for loan administration activities within the structured transaction. Although these activities are often bifurcated or subcontracted, performance accountability to the certificate holders and others involved with the securitization usually rests with the master servicer. The purpose of this Chapter is to explain the CMBS servicer's new and expanded duties that have evolved from the traditional role.

Commercial Servicing Standards

The evolving role of the CMBS servicer is market driven at the present time and is likely to remain market driven for the next several years. There is no government agency, regulatory body, or strong industry-sponsored trade group that is promulgating CMBS servicing requirements; however, several upstart industry associations have made important contributions in an effort to organize and standardize CMBS servicing. At this point, though, there is no manual of generally accepted CMBS servicing standards.

Servicers, particularly master servicers, agree to service pools of securitized commercial loans in accordance with specific pooling and servicing agreements negotiated on each transaction. These agreements, usually hundreds of pages long, have taken the monitoring and reporting role of the servicer to levels never seen before. Servicing responsibilities can vary widely from agreement to agreement; however, general duties and routine activities are not detailed. Reference is typically made to a defined "servicing standard," which simply requires servicers to administer CMBS loans in the same manner in which they administer comparable loans in their own portfolios or in portfolios placed with institutional investors. Fannie Mae and Freddie Mac multifamily servicing guides may be identified to help define the general servicing standard.

What is specifically detailed in the pooling and servicing agreement is the servicer's obligations with respect to the other parties including the trustee, underwriter, special servicer, subservicers, rating agencies, and certificate holders directly involved with the transaction. These specific obligations are usually unique to CMBS servicing and primarily pertain to reporting, remitting, approving, and default administration activities.

■ CMBS Servicer's Customers

The traditional commercial servicer has two primary customers: the investor and the borrower. Investors in commercial real estate mortgage loans have traditionally been banks, savings and loan associations, insurance companies, pension funds, government or government sponsored agencies, private individuals, and investment funds. Although the interests and objectives of the borrowers and investors were often in conflict, particularly in the event of default, the servicer could simply confer with an investor representative whenever the loan documents or law did not specifically address an issue. The close servicer/investor relationship and approval process are important parts of traditional commercial mortgage servicing.

The narrow focus of servicing the borrower on one end of the mortgage loan cycle and the investor at the other evaporates under securitization. The close servicer/investor relationship also disappears. The CMBS servicer is placed in a fiduciary capacity of servicing and administering the loans on behalf of the trust and for the benefit of the certificate holders (the investors). Anyone with the financial resources could potentially be a CMBS certificate holder in the secondary market, although most CMBS bonds are being purchased by large, sophisticated investors at this point in time. What this means is that the CMBS servicer owes a duty of care to those who have or may have a beneficial interest in the cash flows produced by the trust fund. While contractually reporting to the trustee under the pooling and servicing agreement, the servicer also has an indirect responsibility to the other parties to the contracts, the rating agencies, and seemingly limitless numbers of certificate holders and potential certificate holders.

This "many masters" environment, which the CMBS servicer signs up for when it agrees to service a transaction, effectively restricts alternatives in certain decision-making situations. No longer can the servicer call a single investor and obtain approvals, waivers, or decisions on issues that conflict with the loan documents or simply were not addressed in the documents. The CMBS servicer must strictly administer the loans in compliance with the loan and trust documents, which ideally should accommodate every possible situation that could arise with respect to the loan, borrower, or real estate.

Of course, this is rarely, if ever, the case. CMBS pools are typically comprised of varied and often complicated mortgage loans collateralized by unique pieces of real estate. To expect the pooling and servicing agreement and the related investor sales documents (such as the prospectus, offering circular, and private placement memorandum) to accommodate every possible servicing scenario is not realistic. The CMBS servicer inevitably will have to make judgments and decisions based on industry standards and the best interests of the collective certificate holders. It is not practical to solicit the advice or approval from the many certificate holders who may have conflicting interests in the outcome of the decision. Recent CMBS transactions have partially bridged the communication/approval gap between servicer and certificate holder by providing for an operating advisor, a representative of the controlling interest, or certain classes of certificate holders. However, the operating advisor, usually an elected agent, primarily interfaces with the special servicer on specific default administration situations.

■ Servicing Bifurcation

The concept of servicing bifurcation is new to CMBS servicing. The idea of carving up specific servicing responsibilities and activities among the master servicers, subservicers, special servicers, and subcontractors has been in practice for many years on the single-family side of mortgage servicing companies. The Resolution Trust Company (RTC) played an important role in servicing bifurcation as it created large pools of commercial loans from the portfolios of failed financial institutions and introduced the special servicer to administer foreclosures and liquidations of underlying real estate collateral. Wall Street investment banks, particularly those that sponsor REMIC programs, have broken up certain servicing activities even further.

The basic premise underlying bifurcation in the CMBS servicing arena is that there is a central, controlling servicing entity (possibly even the trustee) that is ultimately responsible for all servicing activities; all information, cash receipts, and disbursements should flow or be captured through this entity. The industry has defined this entity as the master servicer, although many pooling and servicing agreements still use the more general term "servicer." There can be only one database, one source of information, and one accounting of cash activity and advances as reports and funds are passed through the trustee on the way to the certificate holders. This means that the bifurcated servicers must report directly to the master servicer on strict schedules throughout the servicing cycle.

The most common form of bifurcation is the subservicer/master servicer relationship. The subservicer, often called the direct servicer or primary servicer, has the front-line relationship with the borrower. The subservicer processes mortgage payments; responds to borrower requests; inspects the property and analyzes rent rolls, leases, and financial statements; pays taxes and insurance, and usually makes the initial contact and collection calls in the event of default. All these activities are monitored or approved by the master servicer. The master servicer reserves the right to step in and assume full servicing responsibilities under certain circumstances (usually a borrower default or subservicer breach). Subservicers are very often the loan originators in conduit programs in which they have been allowed to continue to service for borrower relationship and revenue purposes. Most subservicers are not a party to the pooling and servicing agreement. The specific duties are subcontracted through a separate subservicing agreement, which is provided for or acknowledged in the pooling and servicing agreement.

Many CMBS transactions also employ a special servicer who typically is a party to the pooling and servicing agreement. The concept of the special servicer was used extensively by the RTC in CMBS deals in the early 1990s. The role of the special servicer is one of default and asset administration. Certain event-of-default or "trigger" events are identified in the pooling and servicing agreement. These events, including monetary and nonmonetary defaults under the note and security agreements, as well as other specific events, such as borrower requests for loan modification or forbearance, would prompt the master servicer to transfer certain servicing responsibilities to the special servicer until the event of default is cured. The special servicer would be responsible for delinquency collection efforts, loan modification, forbearance and workout agreements, property inspections, foreclosure and bankruptcy processing, and liquidation of the real estate collateral. Timely communication between the master and special servicer is critical. The master servicer continues to perform certain servicing functions, such as escrow administration, and must funnel information and funds from the special servicer through to the trustee and certificate holders.

Another, more recent form of servicing bifurcation is the concept of a property servicer. In this arrangement, the master servicer delegates the collateral monitoring and analysis activities to a Commercial Real Estate (CRE) specialist, usually someone outside the pooling and servicing agreement. The property servicer's responsibilities include periodic property inspections, quarterly and annual operating statement analysis, and lease and rent roll reviews. The information collected is forwarded to the master servicer, who feeds it into a database for compilation and dissemination. The property servicer is often the special servicer also and eventually may be a certificate holder or may represent one or more classes of certificate holders.

Master servicers also subcontract many of their contractual servicing responsibilities to specialists. Activities such as property inspections, appraisals, engineering studies, environmental surveys, market studies, and title research are often more effectively performed by local experts and industry specialists.

■ Information Requirements of CMBS Servicers

The emergence of the CMBS product has created an intense demand for loan, borrower, and collateral information in the capital markets. Single-family MBS investors have been content over the years to receive summary information about the performance of the bond's underlying loans. This is partly because single-family MBSs are collateralized by many, relatively homogenous, low-balance loans. In most cases, the individual loans carry mortgage insurance, and therefore, if the pool is large enough, no individual loan default will have a significant impact on the cash flows to the undivided interests of the investors. However, this is not necessarily the case with pools of commercial loans. In CMBS transactions, there are far fewer loans that can be collateralized by a wide variety of real estate. A single large commercial loan can easily represent a significant percentage of the overall pool.

A commercial mortgage loan is actually a business loan collateralized by a piece of real estate. Traditional commercial servicers have always kept track of both the performance of the business and the condition of the collateral; these data and analyses have been maintained internally and provided only to the note holder on a periodic basis. The note holder, typically a financial institution, life insurance company, pension fund, government agency, or private investment fund, probably originally underwrote the loan and actively monitors the collateral. Most CMBS investors do not have the time or resources to review or underwrite each commercial loan in a pool, nor can they be expected to monitor the ongoing performance of the loan and collateral through direct contact and site visits like a whole loan investor can. The CMBS structure, due diligence, underwriting, rating, and disclosure process is intended to reduce the need for investor review and analysis.

CMBS investors, particularly below-investment-grade bond buyers, do not make important real estate investment decisions based solely on a rating agency analysis. They also require timely, detailed information and reports about the loans and collateral. CMBS servicers are being asked to collect, maintain, and disseminate an expanding range of information on borrowers, loans, and properties.

Servicers, particularly master servicers in structured transactions, are the funnels through which all information flows. They are the keepers of the activity, history, and database information, which is vital to existing and prospective investors. These investors are restricted from directly accessing loan-level information because they are security holders, not note holders. The challenge for the CMBS servicers is to determine what information should be provided, who is entitled to it, and how to disseminate it in a manner that is consistent with the securities acts and federal regulations.

The requirement to collect and electronically capture additional loan-level and property-level information is a direct result of investor demands that are now emanating from the public, rather than the private, sector. An informed investor always has an advantage over an uninformed investor.

To satisfy initial and subsequent investors of CMBS bonds, investment bankers are constantly expanding the list of data required on each new transaction. To comply and compete, servicers have improved the way information is captured, processed, analyzed, and communicated. Technological enhancements have aided servicer efforts in this area. Most large CMBS servicers now use one of several sophisticated commercial-loan-servicing software systems. To respond to the CMBS "moving target" of information requirements, these commercial software vendors have worked with the servicers to enhance their systems.

Once the information is captured and analyzed, the CMBS servicer must then determine what information is appropriate to release, to whom it should be released, and what communication medium should be employed. This is where borrower's right-to-privacy and insider-information issues collide with the securities laws and the success of the CMBS secondary markets. The CMBS servicer may have a fiduciary duty to borrowers not to disclose the intimate details of their loans, properties, creditworthiness, personal financial conditions, and tenants. This information could be used against the borrowers by their competitors, creditors, and others. However, this same information may be pertinent to an investor's decision about whether or not to purchase the CMBS.

There is very little case law to guide servicers as to what information can be disclosed without incurring liability under the security exchange acts or federal regulations. Rule 10b-5, under the Securities Exchange Act of 1934, appears to be the most menacing because it prohibits "any manipulative or deceptive device or contrivance," as well as the employment of any scheme to defraud in connection with the purchase or sale of any security. It also requires that a material misrepresentation or omission must have been made, which in itself would not make the accurate, complete, and timely disclosure of information to the public illegal under the Act. However, Rule 10b-5 is also the basis for the prohibition on inside trading or tipping.

Although there are compelling arguments as to why Rule 10b-5 does not apply to a CMBS servicer that does not trade in related securities, the application has not been tested in the courts. At this point, CMBS servicers should be cautious and should take steps to mitigate potential future liability under the securities acts, the Fair Credit Reporting Act, the Right to Financial Privacy Act, and other acts that were intended primarily to protect single-family borrowers, but that may have commercial interpretations.

■ Approval Programs for CMBS Servicers

CMBSs are sold to investors as bonds that can be retraded in the secondary market. These bonds are in the form of various tranches that are structured by the investment bank and carry specific quality/risk ratings assigned by one or more rating agencies. Ratings usually range from an AAA, which represents the highest quality, least risky tranche, to a B or an unrated tranche, which represents the most risky, or "first loss," piece.

As a result of the assignment and subsequent surveillance (and the possible upgrading or downgrading of the CMBS bonds), rating agencies are very interested in the qualifications, ability, and experience of the ongoing servicer. Three of the four major CMBS rating agencies, Standard and Poor's, Fitch Investors Services, and Duff & Phelps, have developed formal servicer-evaluation programs and ratings systems or approval lists. Moody's Investors Service reviews the servicer in connection with each specific CMBS transaction on which it rates bonds, but Moody's will not issue a specific report or rating on the servicer.

Although there is some overlap in the rating agencies' definitions, servicers are rated or approved as servicers, master servicers, or special servicers. Servicers have primary borrower-contact and collateral-contact responsibility. Master servicers assume direct-servicing responsibility, possibly through subservicers; they also provide program enhancement in the form of advancing, cash management, and information collection, analysis, and dissemination. Special servicers handle default administration and collateral-liquidation activities.

The rating agencies, through a combination of site visits and research, perform a comprehensive assessment of the servicer's management, organization, loan administration, asset management, and financial position. A rating agency's approval through the evaluation and rating process is a prerequisite to becoming a servicer in a CMBS transaction rated by that agency.

■ Servicing Transfers

Prior to the emergence of CMBS servicing, sales and transfers of commercial servicing rights and responsibilities were rare and usually restricted to government and agency-owned or guaranteed products, such as groups of HUD, Ginnie Mae, Fannie Mae, or Freddie Mac multifamily loans. These were the only types of commercial loans for which a sufficient volume of relatively homogenous loans and servicing characteristics could be assembled in such a way as to make economic sense to sell. Selling individual commercial loans or a group of varying types of commercial loans with different loan terms, servicing requirements, and investors is not practical because the costs associated with negotiating and executing the transfer often exceed the economic benefit to the purchasing servicer.

The CMBS structure has forced more standardization in loan terms, property characteristics, and servicing standards. It has also created one investor reporting and remittance cycle within a transaction. The stated servicing-fee annuity to which the CMBS servicer is entitled is considered to be owned by the servicer. The subservicer or master servicer may have the contractual right to the fees and ancillary income by virtue of having originated the loan or having actually purchased the servicing rights. Most pooling and servicing agreements allow at least the subservicing rights to be sold or simply transferred, usually subject to the approval of the master servicer; however, most prohibit or restrict the transfer of master-servicing rights. The market has already seen a large number of both CMBS subservicing and master servicing transfers as a result of standardization.

■ Summary

This Chapter looked at how the emergence of a secondary market for commercial mortgage-backed securities (CMBSs) has changed the role of the commercial servicer.

The CMBS servicer is in a fiduciary capacity of servicing and administering loans on behalf of the trust and for the benefit of the investors or certificate holders. The narrow focus of servicing the borrower and investor evaporated under commercial securitization. Additionally, the intimate servicer/investor relationship also disappeared.

The concept of bifurcation is new to CMBS servicing. The basic premise is that there is one controlling entity responsible for all servicing activities—generally called the master servicer. The most common form of bifurcation is the subservicer/servicer relationship. The special servicer administers loan default and asset administration. The property servicer handles the collateral monitoring and analysis of activities.

The emergence of CMBS products has increased the demand for loan borrower and collateral information in the capital market. To help insure that investors are informed appropriately about CMBS activity, most of the CMBS rating agencies have developed formal servicer-evaluation programs and rating services for approval purposes.

Most pooling and servicing agreements allow at least subservicing rights to be sold or transferred with master servicer approval. Conversely, most agreements prohibit or restrict the transfer of master-servicing rights.

■ Chapter 11 Review Questions

1. By servicing and administering loans on behalf of the trust and for the benefit of investors, CMBS servicers act in what type of capacity?

   a. Trustorial

   b. Fiduciary

   c. Bifurcative

   d. Intermediary

2. Who is responsible for bridging the communication and approval gap between the CMBS servicer and certificate holders?

   a. Trustee

   b. Intermediary

   c. Fiduciary agent

   d. Operating advisor

3. Which type of servicer handles default and asset administration?

   a. Master

   b. Special

   c. Remedial

   d. Delinquency

4. In the CMBS servicing arena, the use of a central controlling entity who is ultimately responsible for all servicing activities is based on the premise of

   a. bifurcation.

   b. lateralization.

   c. centralization.

   d. intermediation.

5. Although CMBS servicers have a fiduciary duty to _____ not to disclose details of their loans, properties and finances, this same information may be crucial to _____ when deciding to acquire CMBSs.

   a. investors/borrowers

   b. borrowers/investors

   c. trustees/investors

   d. borrowers/trustees

6. Commercial software vendors have been working with CMBS servicers to respond to their information requirements which are best described as which type of approach?

   a. Potpourri

   b. Hit or miss

   c. Topsy turvy

   d. Moving target

7. Which rating agency does *NOT* have a formal CMBS servicer-evaluation program?

   a. Standard & Poor's

   b. Duff & Phelps

   c. Fitch Investors Services

   d. Moody's Investors Service

8. Which type of responsibility is assumed by master servicers of CMBSs?

   a. Subservicing

   b. Administration

   c. Direct-servicing

   d. Dissemination

9. Prior to the emergence of CMBS servicing, the sales and transfers of commercial servicing rights were rare.

   a. True

   b. False

10. Which rights do most CMBS pooling and servicing agreements allow to be sold or transferred?

    a. Special

    b. Servicing

    c. Operating

    d. Subservicing

Chapter 1 Review Questions

1. *1* Communicates well
   2 Delegate responsibilities
   3 Deal effectively and efficiently with borrowers
   4 Follow through to ensure quality and accuracy
2. *b* False
3. *b*
4. *a*
5. *1* Loan-based
   2 Function-based
6. *a*

Chapter 2 Review Questions

1. *b*
2. *a* True
3. *a*
4. *b*
5. *b*
6. *a*
7. *b*
8. *a* True
9. *1* Check
   2 Wire transfer
10. *c*

Chapter 3 Review Questions

1. *1* Direct billing
   2 Coupon book
2. *b*
3. *d*
4. *b*
5. *d*
6. *b* False
7. *c*
8. *d*

Chapter 4 Review Questions

1. *c*
2. *d*
3. *1* Rent insurance
   2 Umbrella liability
   3 Boiler and machinery
   4 Fire, extended coverage, and vandalism
4. *a*
5. *e*
6. *a*
7. *a*
8. *d*
9. *c*
10. *a*
11. *a* True
12. *a*

Chapter 5 Review Questions

1. *b* False
2. *b*
3. *1* Defaults
   2 Demised premises
   3 Rent payments
   4 Tenant contributions
   5 Condemnation clause
4. *d*
5. *1* Radius clause
   2 Parking regulations
   3 Continuous occupancy
   4 Merchant's association
   5 Advertising and graphics
6. *c*
7. *b, a, c*
8. *d*
9. *c*
10. *b*

Chapter 6 Review Questions

1. *d*
2. *b*
3. *b*
4. *a*
5. *c*
6. *1, 3, 5, 2, 4*

Chapter 7 Review Questions

1. *1* Credit information on purchaser
   2 Resumé of proposed purchaser
   3 Copy of executed sales contract
   4 Short-term and long-term management plans of purchaser
2. *c*
3. *b*
4. *b*
5. *1* If the loan can be prepaid
   2 The existence of due dates for prepayment penalties
   3 Any miscellaneous terms and conditions that may affect payoff or pre-payment
   4 If written notice within a specified time period is required of the borrower
6. *a* True

Chapter 8 Review Questions

1. *b*
2. *c*
3. *a*
4. *d*
5. *b*
6. *d*

Chapter 9 Review Questions

1. *d*
2. *a*
3. *1* Market
   2 Borrower capabilities
   3 Property characteristics
4. *b* False
5. *b*
6. *b*
7. *a, d, c, b*
8. *a*

Chapter 10 Review Questions

1. *b*
2. *b* False
3. *a*
4. *d*
5. *c*
6. *b*
7. *d*
8. *1, 2, 3, 4*
9. *1* Due diligence review
   2 Operations analysis
   3 Method of acquisition
   4 Problem identification and approach
   5 Directing and scheduling foreclosures
10. *d*
11. *d*
12. *c*
13. *d*
14. *b*

Chapter 11 Review Questions

1. *b*
2. *d*
3. *b*
4. *a*
5. *b*
6. *d*
7. *d*
8. *c*
9. *a* True
10. *d*

a-pieces Refers to security classes (tranches) rated as investment grade for institutional investors; can also include the class rated BBB, as that is considered an investment grade for most regulated institutions; also called senior pieces.

abatement (rental) A reduction or elimination of rent payments for a specified period of time, usually granted by the landlord as an inducement to the tenant to enter into or to renew a lease.

abatement (tax) A reduction in real property tax granted by a taxing authority as the result of an appeal. In some jurisdictions, tax abatements may also be granted as an inducement for development or to attract or retain job-providing industries.

ACES *See* alternative credit enhancement structure.

absorption rate The rate at which vacant space is either leased or sold to users in the market place. Absorption rate is usually expressed in square feet per year or, in the case of multifamily housing, number of units per year.

acceleration clause A common provision of a mortgage that allows the holder to demand the entire outstanding mortgage balance due and payable in the event of a breach of the mortgage contract.

accident Unplanned, unexpected, and undesigned event that occurs suddenly at a definite place. *See* occurrence.

accounts payable Money owed by a business to suppliers of goods and services. Accounts payable are considered current liabilities on the balance sheet.

accounts receivable Money owed to a business for goods or services provided to customers. Accounts receivable are classified as current assets on the balance sheet, with a contra account for bad debts on receivables.

ACH (Automatic Clearing House) A computer-based facility for interchange of electronic entries between financial institutions.

ACORD form A form utilized by the insurance industry for use between an **A**gency and a **C**ompany for **O**rganization, **R**esearch, and **D**evelopment.

actual cash value Valuation of damaged property that allows for depreciation.

ADA compliance Compliance with the provisions of the **A**mericans with **D**isabilities **A**ct that establishes minimum requirements for facilities with public access to accommodate physically handicapped persons.

additional insured Individual, business, or organization covered by a policy in addition to the named insured.

admitted insurer Insurance company licensed to do business in a certain jurisdiction.

advances Payments made by the servicer on delinquent loans. In addition to principal and interest, advances can be required for property protection, taxes, insurance, and foreclosure costs. The servicer has a proxy claim to subsequent collections and foreclosure proceeds as reimbursement for advances up to an amount that was determined recoverable. Servicers do not have to advance fees that are deemed nonrecoverable by the trustee or an officer of the servicers. Servicers are usually paid prime plus 1 percent for their advances.

agency securities Securities issued by government or quasi-government agencies such as Fannie Mae and Freddie Mac.

aggregate deductible A provision whereby the policyholder agrees to self-assume the payment of claims incurred up to a specific amount or limit, with the insurer paying all claims after such limit is attached.

aggregate limit of liability A provision which limits the maximum liability of an insurer for losses in a given time period (usually 12 months). Policy limits are usually expressed in maximums per accident (or occurrence), with an aggregate for all losses in any one year.

agreed amount An agreement whereby the coinsurance clause is waived if the insured agrees to carry a specific amount of insurance which represents at least 90 percent to 100 percent of total values at risk. Also known as *stated amount coinsurance.*

agreed amount endorsement An insurance endorsement used with a policy containing a coinsurance clause. It binds the insurance company to an agreement that the amount of insurance carried under the policy is sufficient to meet the requirements of the coinsurance clause in the policy. Addition of the agreed amount endorsement eliminates the risk of the coinsurance penalty.

all-cash offer A proposal to purchase property without any contingency to obtain a loan to finance any portion of the purchase price.

all-in cost The term applied to the total costs of a securitization; usually quoted in basis points to reflect what the costs would have added to yield if they had not been spent on the creation of the security.

alternative credit enhancement structure (ACES) A program created by Fannie Mae to provide liquidity to the multifamily CMBS market.

amenity A feature that enhances property value. Examples are off-street reserved parking within a condominium community, the proximity of public transportation, tennis courts, or a swimming pool.

American Council of Life Insurance (ACLI) The ACLI collects data from life insurance companies regarding their portfolios. The ACLI has information on approximately 87 percent of all mortgages held by life insurance companies.

amortization Repayment of a mortgage debt with periodic payments of both principal and interest, calculated to retire the obligation at the end of a fixed period of time.

anchor tenant A prime tenant in a shopping center, such as an established department store, that attracts the bulk of customers to the center.

appraisal An opinion or estimate of value. Also refers to the process by which a value estimate is obtained.

appraiser One qualified by education, training, and experience to estimate the value of real and personal property.

arm's length transaction A transaction in which the parties involved are entirely independent of each other, deal with each other as strangers, and have no reason for collusion.

asbestos Insulating, fire-resistant, and heat-resistant material commonly used in insulation and roofing.

assessment A value factor assigned to real property and used to determine real property taxes. The process of reaching the assessed valuation. Also, an add-on tax to raise money for a special purpose.

asset A property or right owned, tangible or intangible, that has monetary value and is capable of providing future benefits to its owner.

assignment of lease A mortgage clause that passes control of leases on an income producing property to the lender; often a condition to making a loan to ensure, in the case of mortgage default, that any continuing income from the property goes directly to the lender.

assignment of rents A transfer to the mortgagee of the right to collect rents from tenants in the event of default by the property owner.

assignment The transfer of ownership rights, or interests in property, as in a mortgage, lease, or deed of trust.

assumption A buyer's acceptance of primary liability for payment of the existing note secured by a mortgage or deed of trust.

assumption agreement A written agreement by one party to pay an obligation originally incurred by another.

assumption fee The amount paid a lender for the paperwork and processing of records necessary to approve and document a new debtor.

attornment agreement A letter acknowledging a new owner as a landlord or a new organization as a loan servicer.

audit The official examination and verification of bookkeeping accounts to prove the accuracy of figures and the adequacy of accounting controls. An audit may be done by public accountants hired for this purpose or by a company's own employees. The latter is called an *internal audit*.

available funds All funds available or collected including prepayments and servicer advances.

b-piece A term applied to the classes (tranches) of CMBSs rated "BB" and lower. Also called below investment grade (BIG) by regulated institutional investors.

back-up The process of taking all data stored on the computer and copying it onto tapes, or another storage medium, so it can be shipped to another location for safe keeping.

balance sheet A report of the financial position of a business at a specific point in time, showing its assets, liabilities, and owner's equity.

balloon mortgage A mortgage with periodic installments of principal and interest that do not fully amortize the loan. The balance of the mortgage is due in a lump sum at a specified date usually at the end of the term.

balloon risk The risk that a borrower is unable to make a balloon payment at maturity.

bankruptcy Court proceedings to relieve the debts of an individual or business unable to pay its creditors.

base rent The minimum fixed guaranteed rent in a commercial property lease.

base stop The maximum amount of building operating expenses that will be borne by the landlord prior to passing additional amounts through to the tenant. The base stop is expressed as an absolute dollar amount or dollar per square foot amount.

base year Similar to *base stop*, except that rather than being specified as an absolute amount, the landlord's expenses are limited to the amount incurred in a specified calendar or fiscal year, usually (but not always) the calendar year in which the lease commences.

basis point 0.001 percent (one one-hundredth of one percent). Used primarily to describe changes in yield or price on debt instruments, including mortgages and mortgage-backed securities.

basis risk Refers to the risk of the underlying mortgage loans and offered certificates tied to different indices. It is the possibility of the certificate accruing interest at higher interest rates than the underlying mortgage loans. When the aggregate amount of interest on the certificates is greater than the collateral, the amount is known as the basis-risk shortfall.

bid The price at which a seller will sell particular securities. In the security and commodity trade, the highest price offered for a security or commodity at a given time; also, a "quotation" or "quote."

binder A legal agreement issued by the insurer or it's agent to provide evidence of coverage until such time as a full policy(ies) can be issued.

bodily injury liability insurance Protection against loss arising out of the liability imposed upon the insured by law for damages due to bodily injury, sickness, or disease sustained by third parties. *See* personal injury.

boiler and machinery insurance Coverage for the loss to boilers and machinery caused by explosion or mechanical breakdown. The policy may cover damage to the boilers, machinery, other property, and business interruption.

bona fide A Latin term meaning *in good faith*, without fraud.

book value The capitalized cost of an asset, less depreciation taken for accounting purposes, based on the method used for the computing of depreciation over the useful life of the asset. The actual value of an asset after deducting depreciation and all liabilities is the net book value.

borrower One who receives funds in the form of a loan with the obligation of repaying the loan in full with interest.

borrower/guarantor full recourse An agreement wherein the borrower/guarantor has personally agreed to fully repay all amounts owed under a mortgage loan, irrespective of whether the collateral is adequate to retire the debt. This agreement gives the holder of the note, or other negotiable instrument, the right to recover against the borrower/guarantor personally, including any and all assets of the borrower/guarantor.

borrower/guarantor partial recourse An agreement wherein the borrower/guarantor has personally agreed to repay a set dollar amount, all amounts exceeding a stated dollar amount, or a percentage of the outstanding balance of the mortgage loan. This agreement gives the holder of the note, or other negotiable instrument, the right to recover against the borrower/guarantor personally, including any and all assets of the borrower/guarantor, but *only* to the extent specified. For example, a borrower/guarantor may agree to pay the first $1 million of a $5 million loan or the top 25 percent of the loan.

breakpoint In a retail lease, the point specified in absolute sales dollars or sales dollars per square foot, above which the tenant has agreed to pay percentage rent in addition to base rent. For example, in addition to base rent, a tenant may agree to pay 2 percent of annual gross sales above $2 million. In this case, $2 million is the breakpoint.

broad form A term used to describe coverage that extends beyond "standard" peril insurance policies, i.e., fire and extended coverage, named perils, etc.

broad form property damage An endorsement to a general liability policy that grants expanded coverage to property in the care, custody, or control of the insured, property that is not normally insured if damaged by the insured's negligence.

builder's risk insurance Fire and extended coverage insurance for a building under construction. Coverage increases automatically as the building progresses and terminates at completion.

building code Regulations based on safety and health standards that govern design, construction, and materials used in construction.

business interruption insurance Compensation to a business owner or operator for income lost when the business is closed due to fire or any other insured hazard.

call option A provision of a note that allows the lender the right to demand or "call in" the balance of the obligation. The call can be exercised due to a breach of specified terms or conditions, or at the discretion of the lender (such as when the note rate is lower than the current market rate).

CAM expenses *See* common area maintenance.

capital improvement Any structure or component erected as a permanent improvement to real property that adds to its value and useful life.

capital improvement reserves Reserves may be required by loan documents to fund the future payment of capital improvement for the property.

capitalization The conversion of a future net income stream into present value by using a specific desired rate of earnings as a discount rate.

capitalization analysis The analysis based on the conversion of a future net income stream into present value by using a specific desired rate of earnings as a discount rate.

capitalization rate The rate of return on net operating income considered acceptable for an investor and used to determine the capitalized value. This rate should provide a return on, as well as a return of, capital. Also known as *cap rate*.

cash flow (after taxes) Cash received less cash paid out, including income taxes paid.

cash flow (before taxes) Cash received less cash paid out, before any consideration for income taxes.

cash-flow modeling When pools of loans are converted to securities, all payments, including balloon maturities, are chronologically collated into a cash flow pool and then sequentially allocated to the various classes of securities created with the issuance of a CMBS.

cash reserve Reserves normally kept by the owner of the property to fund any operating shortfall or capital improvements that are required for the property.

casualty or theft loss Losses on property arising from fire, storm, theft, or similar sudden and unexpected occurrences.

central business district (CBD) The area geographically located within the central business district of a municipality.

certificates of insurance A form that evidences policy coverage, limits, etc., and is generally used as proof of insurance. These forms have no legal status and cannot be used in lieu of actual insurance policies.

claims made Policies written on a "claims made" basis only cover claims presented during the particular year the policy is in force, for incidents that occurred during the same policy year, or for any previous year noted in the "claims made" policy (retroactive date). This form of coverage contrasts with an "occurrence" policy that responds to incidents regardless of when the claim is reported.

closed (exclusive) listing The right of one agent to be the only one, other than the owner, who may sell the property during a period of time.

closed period The interval of time under a mortgage during which the loan cannot be prepaid.

closing In real estate, the delivery of a deed, financial adjustments, the signing of a note, and the disbursement of funds necessary to consummate a sale or loan transaction.

closing statement A financial disclosure giving an account of all funds received and expected at closing, including escrow deposits for taxes, hazard insurance, and mortgage insurance. All FHA, VA, and most conventionally financed loans use a uniform settlement statement called the "HUD-1."

coinsurance A clause that forces an insured to share in a loss if he/she is underinsured at the time of the loss. For a reduced premium, the insured is obligated to carry an amount of insurance to a specified minimal level, usually prescribed to be a fixed percentage of the value of the insured property. Failure of the insured to insure to that level results in a penalty in payout equal to the amount deficient.

collateral Property pledged as security for a debt, for example, mortgaged real estate.

collateral valuation process The process by which a property's price is determined.

commercially reasonable Fair, proper, just, or suitable under generally accepted business (commercial) standards or circumstances.

commingling Combining funds (such as escrows) into one account that should be accounted for and deposited into separate accounts.

commission An agent's compensation for negotiating a real estate or loan transaction, often expressed as a percentage of the selling price.

commitment An agreement, often in writing, between a lender and a borrower, to loan money at a future date, subject to specified conditions.

In secondary marketing, an agreement, in writing, between a lender and an investor to buy and sell mortgages under specific terms.

common area An area owned by the owners or tenants of a complex or subdivision, for the common use of residents.

common area maintenance expenses (CAM expenses) Expenses associated with the maintenance of the common areas.

comparables Properties used for comparative purposes in the appraisal process that have characteristics similar to the subject property. Also, "comps."

comprehensive general liability insurance A policy that covers a variety of general liability exposures, including premises, property, and operations, products liability, owner's and contractor's protective, contractual liability, elevator liability, and employer's liability.

concessions A discount or other inducement given by a landlord or seller to a prospective tenant or buyer to induce them to sign a lease or purchase property.

condemnation The taking of private property for public use under the right to eminent domain with just compensation paid the owner and others with an interest in the condemned property.

consideration Something of value offered and accepted in exchange for a promise, without which an agreement is unenforceable.

constant Percentage of the original loan paid in equal annual payments that provides principal reduction and interest payments over the life of the loan. For example, a $1 million loan with a 10.8 percent constant requires a $108,000 annual payment.

construction loan A short-term, interim loan for financing the cost of construction. The lender advances funds to the builder at periodic intervals as work progresses.

construction loan agreement A written agreement between a lender and a builder and/or borrower that details the specific terms and conditions of a construction loan, including the schedule of payments.

construction loan draw A partial disbursement of the construction loan based on the schedule of payments in the loan agreement. Also, "takedown."

construction costs All costs incurred in the completion of a construction project, including land, labor, overhead, and builder's profit.

contingency A clause in a contract that requires the completion of a certain act or the occurrence of a certain event.

contingency reserve A reserve account in which funds are held until certain specified conditions are satisfied.

contract An agreement between two or more parties which creates an obligation to do or not to do a particular thing.

contractor A person or company who agrees to do work and/or furnish materials for a contracted price. Subcontractors are often hired by the contractor to perform specialized or technical labor.

corporate resolutions The affirmative and formal action by the board of directors of a corporation approving a transaction, activity, or decision.

cost approach to value A valuation approach in which the value of a property is determined by computing the replacement value of improvements, depreciation, and the value of land.

cost overrun The amount of money required or expended over and above budgeted cost, including such items as labor, interest, materials, and land.

covenant A legally enforceable promise or restriction in a mortgage. For example, the borrower may covenant to keep the property in good repair and adequately insured against fire and other casualties. A breach of covenant in a mortgage usually creates a default as defined by the mortgage, and can be the basis for foreclosure.

credit Financial status—ability of borrower to meet the terms of his obligations.

cross-defaulting clause A clause in some mortgage agreements that states a default by the borrower on one mortgage loan also triggers a default on the other loan stated in the clause.

current asset ratio The ratio of current assets to current liabilities.

cycle (economic) A period of time, such as when the economy is growing or when it is in a recession.

date-down title insurance endorsement An instrument, provided by the title company, indicating that no liens have been placed on the property since its original issuance of the title insurance policy, or since any prior date-down endorsement.

debris removal A property policy extension of coverage that grants coverage for the expense of removing debris caused by damage to property by an insured peril. Property should be defined as both insured and uninsured.

debt/equity ratio The proportion of capital borrowed to the amount of capital invested out-of-pocket or obtained through the sale of common stock. Also, "leverage ratio."

debt service A borrower's periodic mortgage payments comprised of principal and/or interest on the unpaid mortgage balance.

debt service coverage ratio A ratio of effective annual net operating income to annual principal and/or interest payments. Also, "debt service coverage."

deed The document by which title to real property is transferred or conveyed from one party to another.

deed of trust A type of security instrument in which the borrower conveys title to real property to a third party (trustee) to be held in trust as security for the lender, with the provision that the trustee shall reconvey the title upon the payment of the debt, and, conversely, will sell the land and pay the debt in the event of a default by the borrower. *See* mortgage.

deed-in-lieu A deed given by a borrower/mortgagor to a lender/mortgagee to satisfy a debt and avoid foreclosure.

default A breach or nonperformance of the terms of a note, the covenants of a mortgage, or the terms of other loan documents.

default interest rate The interest rate stipulated by certain mortgage documents which is triggered by a breach or nonperformance of the terms of a note, the covenants of a mortgage, or the terms of other loan documents.

default letter A letter sent to the borrower indicating that a breach or nonperformance of the terms of a note, the covenants of a mortgage, or the terms of other loan documents has occurred. This letter also advises the borrower of the rights of the lender under the note/mortgage and requires that the default be cured.

deferred maintenance Postponed, infrequent, or inadequate maintenance practices on a building or property, often resulting in physical depreciation and loss of value. Deferred maintenance can be an indicator of inadequate cash flow or lack of pride in the property. Also, "curable depreciation."

delinquency Failure of a borrower to make timely payments specified under a loan agreement.

demand letter Correspondence sent to the borrower indicating that unless the loan is made current within a certain time frame, the lender can, by virtue of a default, declare the entire principal balance outstanding as well as all interest due under the note to be due and payable.

demand note/mortgage A note or mortgage that the lender can call due at any time and without prior notice.

demographics *See* demography.

demography The study of the characteristics of human populations such as size, growth, density, distribution, and vital statistics.

demolition clause Coverage extended to cover the cost of demolishing property damaged by an insured peril. Policies may be extended to cover the cost of demolishing undamaged property made necessary by a bylaw, court order, etc.

density The ratio between total land area and the number of residential or commercial structures placed upon it. Local ordinances usually regulate density.

depreciation A decline in value of a building or other real estate improvement, resulting from age, physical wear, and economic or functional obsolescence. This figure is deducted annually from net income.

direct payment Method of payment wherein a check or other form of consideration is delivered directly to the investor's or servicer's place of business.

disappearing deductible A deductible that disappears as the loss gets larger, i.e., a $500 deductible will not apply to losses over $10,000.

discount In loan originations, a discount refers to an amount withheld from loan proceeds by a lender. In secondary market sales, a discount is the amount by which the sale price of a note is less than its face value. In both instances, the purpose of a discount is to adjust the yield upward, either in lieu of interest or in addition to interest. The rate or amount of discount depends on money market conditions, the credit of the borrower, and the rate or terms of the note.

discount rate The rate of return used to convert expected future cash flows into present dollar value equivalent.

discounted cash-flow analysis (DCF) Method of applying an appropriate discount to cash to be received in the future to arrive at the present value of those future earnings.

distressed property Term that denotes property in trouble due to one of several reasons, such as: cost overrun, insufficient income, poor management, or any other conditions that affect the mortgagor's ability to repay the loan on a timely basis.

divest To release an interest one has in property.

down payment A portion of the sale price paid to a seller by a buyer to close a sales transaction, with the understanding that the balance will be paid at settlement. Also, the difference between the sale price of real estate and the mortgage amount.

draw Periodic advances of funds according to the schedule of payments in a construction loan agreement. Also "advance, disbursement, pay-out, progress payment, or takedown."

due date Date which the borrower must pay the interest and/or the principal due on his or her mortgage, as stated in the note, as well as any escrow payment.

due diligence review An examination by a purchaser of a servicing portfolio. Generally the reviewer will look at credit quality and underwriting of the loan collateral underlying the servicing rights; correctness and completeness of the loan documents; the seller's servicing practices and methodologies; and the accuracy of the portfolio offering document. As used here, a re-underwriting of the loan in line with borrower's request to determine the feasibility of the request by lender.

due-on-encumbrance A provision appearing in a mortgage providing for the acceleration of a loan upon the placement of additional mortgage liens on collateral already pledged/mortgaged to a lender.

due-on-sale A clause in a mortgage stating that if the mortgagor sells, transfers, or in any way encumbers the property, then the mortgagee has the right to implement an acceleration clause making the balance of the obligation due.

easement A right to the limited use or enjoyment of land held by another, including, for example, an interest in land to enable sewer or other utility lines to be laid, or to allow access to a property.

economic or commercial real estate weakness An area exhibiting poor occupancies, low rents, plant or military base closings, or low sales and appraised values.

economic value The condition of the property based on its earning potential.

effective gross income Stabilized income after vacancy and bad debt allowances that a property is expected to generate.

effective rent The rental income generated by a lease computed over the life of the lease and expressed as an annual dollar amount or annual dollar amount per square foot. This figure is typically computed as the aggregate rent to be paid under the lease net of any abated rent and allowances, divided by the term of the lease. However, there has been a trend toward computing effective rent more realistically by using a time-value-of-money calculation. In this latter approach, sometimes called the "equivalent level rent calculation," a market discount rate is applied to all cash flows from the lease to obtain a present value that is then reduced by the cost of any concessions or inducements paid to put the lease in place. The resultant net value is then converted to the equivalent level payment stream that would produce an equivalent net present value at that discount rate.

egress To go out. It is used with the word *ingress* (to go in) to describe the right of access to land.

encroachment An improvement that illegally violates another's property or right to use that property.

encumbrance Anything that affects or limits the fee simple title to property, such as mortgages, leases, easements, or restrictions.

engineer's report A report rendered by an engineer stating the physical condition of property that has been inspected with a summation or recommendation thereof.

environmental impairment insurance A special form of insurance designed to protect an insured against claims for liability and clean-up costs related to pollution. Coverage may be granted for gradual and sudden and accidental pollution, and is always written on a claims made form.

Environmental Protection Agency (EPA) The agency responsible for enforcing environmental liability.

escrow An item of value, money, or documents deposited with a third party to be delivered upon the fulfillment of a condition. For example, the deposit by a borrower with the lender of funds to pay taxes and insurance premiums when they become due, or the deposit of funds or documents with an attorney or escrow agent to be disbursed upon the closing of a sale of real estate. In some parts of the country, escrows of taxes and insurance premiums are called *impounds* or *reserves*.

escrow account The segregated trust account in which escrow funds are held.

escrow analysis The periodic examination of escrow accounts to determine if current monthly deposits will provide sufficient funds to pay taxes, insurance, and other bills when due.

escrow transfer agreement An instrument transferring escrow funds (and obligations under an existing escrow agreement) held by the lender to a third party upon transfer of property.

estoppel certificate A written statement setting forth certain facts which cannot later be repudiated (frequently given by a lender or a tenant relative to a loan or lease, respectively).

excess (positive) cash flow An amount of income derived from the operation of a property or business after deducting or paying all expenses.

excess coverage Coverage designed to be in excess over one or more primary policies that will not pay out until the primary limits of liability are exhausted.

exclusive listing A written contract giving one licensed real estate agent the exclusive right to sell a property for a specified time but reserving the owner's right to sell the property alone without the payment of a commission.

expense stop *See* base stop.

exposure The total amount a lender has tied up in a loan. Usually the outstanding principal balance of the loan plus accrued interest, and any capitalized costs including legal fees and expenses, appraisal and environmental fees, and all other costs associated with securing the lender's interest in the property.

extended coverage A common extension of coverage beyond the normal fire and lightning perils. Damage caused by windstorm, hail, explosion, riot, vehicles, smoke, aircraft, and other falling objects are the additional perils insured by this coverage.

fair market value The price at which property is transferred between a willing buyer and a willing seller, each of whom has a reasonable knowledge of all pertinent facts and neither being under any compulsion to buy or sell.

Fannie Mae (Federal National Mortgage Association) The nation's largest mortgage investor, created in 1968 by an amendment to Title III of the National Housing Act (12 USC 1716 et seq.). This stockholder-owner corporation, a portion of whose board of directors is appointed by the President of the United States, supports the secondary market in mortgages on residential property with mortgage purchase and securitization programs.

Fannie Mae DUS Lender A lender designated by Fannie Mae who originates, underwrites, closes, and services Fannie Mae approved multifamily mortgage loans.

FDIC *See* Federal Deposit Insurance Corporation.

federal bank wire A payment system operated by the Federal Reserve for the transfer of federal funds balances between financial institutions maintaining accounts at U.S. Federal Reserve Banks.

Federal Deposit Insurance Corporation (FDIC) Originally established by the Banking Act of 1933 to protect depositors from loss. As a result of the Financial Institutions Reform, Recovery and Enforcement Act of 1989 (FIRREA), the FDIC administers the Bank Insurance Fund (BIF) and the Savings Association Insurance Fund (SAIF).

Federal Home Loan Mortgage Corporation *See* Freddie Mac.

Federal National Mortgage Association *See* Fannie Mae.

fee simple The greatest possible interest a person can have in real estate, including the right to dispose of the property or pass it on to one's heirs.

FHLMC (Federal Home Loan Mortgage Corporation) *See* Freddie Mac.

fidelity (bond) A type of insurance that generally covers losses caused by dishonest or fraudulent acts by employees and others.

the final rule Attempts to state the circumstance under which lenders would not be deemed "participating in the management" or "influencing" the control, handling, or disposal of hazardous materials at a borrower's property and, therefore, would not be liable for their remediation.

financial statement A financial report, including a balance sheet and an income statement.

financial statement analysis Evaluation of the existing and potential income stream of the real estate to determine prospective cash flow and debt service capacity.

financing statement Under the Uniform Commercial Code (UCC), a prescribed document a lender files with the Recorder of Deeds or Secretary of State, giving the name and address of the debtor and the secured party (lender), along with a description of the personal property securing the loan.

first mortgage A mortgage that gives the mortgagee a security right over all other mortgages of the mortgaged property.

fixture Personal property that becomes real property upon being attached to real estate.

FNMA (Federal National Mortgage Association) *See* Fannie Mae.

flood insurance Insurance that reimburses the policyholder for damage to property caused by the peril of flood.

forbearance The act of refraining from taking legal action despite the fact that the mortgage is in arrears. It is usually granted only when a mortgagor makes satisfactory arrangements to pay the amount owed at a future date.

force majeure insurance A specialized form of coverage for owners and contractors to protect against damage or delays caused by unpredictable events such as war, strikes, or those perils not normally insured under *all risk* policies.

forced placed coverage Hazard coverage obtained by a lender to protect its security interest in a property where the borrower has failed to renew existing coverage. Premiums for this coverage are usually above market rates and most mortgage instruments allow for this premium to be charged to the borrower.

foreclosure A legal procedure in which a mortgaged property is sold in a legal process to pay the outstanding debt in case of default.

Freddie Mac (Federal Home Loan Mortgage Corporation) Created by Congress in Title III of the Emergency Home Finance Act of 1970 (12 USC 1451 et seq.). This stockholder-owned corporation, a portion of whose board of directors is appointed by the President of the United States, supports the secondary market in mortgages on residential and multifamily properties with mortgage purchase and securitization programs.

friable A condition, most frequently utilized in the context of asbestos, where environmental contaminants (usually asbestos fibers) have the potential to become dislodged or disturbed and airborne, thus becoming a threat to one's health.

funding Payment of loan money by a lender to a borrower so that he or she can purchase real estate, or the payment of money by investors to lenders in return for mortgages sold to them by the lender.

generally accepted accounting principles (GAAP) Accounting practices mandated by recognized rule-making authorities.

general contractor A party that performs or supervises the construction or development of a property pursuant to the terms of a primary contract with the owner. The general contractor may use its own employees for this work or the services of other contractors (subcontractors).

grace period A period of time (usually measured in days) after an obligation is due or is to be performed during which a borrower can perform without incurring a penalty and without being considered in default.

gross rate Interest rate on a mortgage, including servicing fees.

groundwater Water in the subsoil.

guarantee An individual's or entity's promise to pay in the event of an operational shortfall.

guarantor A party who is secondarily liable for another's debt or performance (in contrast to a surety, who is primarily liable with the principal debtor).

guaranty A promise by one party to pay a debt or perform an obligation contracted for or by another in the event that the obligor fails to pay or perform as contracted.

hazard insurance Insurance coverage that provides compensation to the insured in case of property loss or damage.

hazard waste risk A financial or health risk that is created due to any substance such as asbestos, urea formaldehyde foam insulation, transformers containing polychlorinated biphenyls (PCBs) in excess of 50 parts per million, lead paint, or any substance deemed hazardous or toxic, or required to be disclosed, reported, treated, removed, disposed of, or cleaned up by any applicable hazardous material law.

highest and best use The use of land that will bring the greatest return.

holdback A portion of a loan commitment not funded until some additional requirement, such as rental or construction completion, is attained. In construction or interim lending, a percentage of the contractor's draw held back to provide additional protection for the interim lender, often an amount equal to the contractor's profit given over when the interim loan is closed.

HVAC The heating, ventilating, and air-conditioning system.

hypothecate To pledge property as security for a debt without giving up possession of title.

income and expense statement The actual or estimated schedule of income and expense items reflecting net gain or loss during a specified period.

income approach to value The appraisal technique used to estimate real property value by capitalizing net income.

indemnify To protect against damage, loss, or injury, or to make compensation to for damage, loss, or injury.

indemnity Security against or compensation for damage, loss, or injury. Also, a legal exemption from liability for damages.

index A published interest rate, such as the prime rate, LIBOR, T-Bill rate, or the 11th District COFI. Lenders use indexes to establish interest rates charged on mortgages or to compare investment returns. On ARMs, a predetermined margin is added to the index to compute the interest rate adjustment.

inflation guard An endorsement to an insurance policy that increases coverage to offset the effects of inflation.

infrastructure Basic public improvements such as roads, sewers, water, drainage, and other utilities that are necessary to prepare raw land for buildings and future development.

ingress To go in. It is used with *egress* (to go out) to describe the right of access to land.

innocent landowner defense A term utilized by an owner of property, including a mortgagee who has taken title to property by judicial proceeding or by deed-in-lieu of foreclosure, in the context of avoiding liability for environmental contamination where the owner has taken certain precautions to ascertain the environmental condition of property prior to acquiring the property.

installment The periodic payment that a borrower agrees to pay a mortgage lender.

insurance vacancy clause A provision in a hazard insurance policy protecting the insured upon the occurrence of property loss or damage, even if the insured property is vacant (for an extended period of time).

insured The term preferred over other terms such as "policyholder" or "policyowner" to describe the party protected under an insurance contract to whom the insurer reimburses losses, pays benefits, or provides services.

intangible property Generally, property that has no intrinsic or marketable value in and of itself but is merely the evidence of value, such as promissory notes, stock certificates, or certificates of deposits (as distinguished from land, furniture, and equipment).

interest reserve A holdback of loan proceeds by a lender to be utilized to pay interest as it accrues on a loan.

interest Consideration in the form of money paid for the use of money, usually expressed as an annual percentage. Also, a "right, share, or title in property."

interest rate Percentage paid for the use of money, usually expressed as an annual percentage.

joint and several note Two or more persons or entities, each of whom is liable for the full amount of the debt.

judgment Final determination by a court of the rights and claims of the parties to an action.

junior lenders (mortgage) A mortgage that is subordinate to the claims of a prior lien or mortgage.

landlord Owner or lessor of real property.

late charge An additional charge that a borrower is required to pay as a penalty for failure to pay a regular installment when due.

lease analysis The formal review of a lease that is usually memorialized in writing on a form which provides details of the business terms and legal issues.

lease audit An official examination and verification of the status of leases (or a lease) to prove or ascertain the lease terms and their adequacy.

lease guaranty An instrument by which an individual or entity guaranties payment and/or performance of the tenant's obligations under the tenant's lease.

lease concessions A grant/concession given by a landlord to a tenant to induce the tenant to execute a lease. An example: period of free or reduced rent or improving the leased premises at the landlord's expense.

lease A written document containing the conditions under which the possession and use of real and/or personal property are given by the owner to another for a stated period and consideration.

lease modification An instrument modifying the original lease and its terms and conditions.

lease summary abstract A brief lease analysis (on a legal basis) which can be recorded.

legal description A property description, recognized by law, that is sufficient to locate and identify the property without oral testimony.

lender Person or entity that invests in or originates loans, such as a mortgage banker, credit union, commercial bank, or savings and loan. In commercial property usage, the lender may be a life insurance company, bank, or pension fund that provides the funds and in whose name the loan is closed.

lender liability An area of legal findings that would hold the lender financially responsible for damages and costs based upon the lender's activities (especially in the management of real estate securing any of the lender's mortgage loans as this relates to environmental clean-up liability).

lessee One holding rights of possession and use of property under the terms of a lease. *See* tenant.

lessor One who leases property to a lessee. *See* landlord.

letter of attornment *See* attornment agreement.

letter of credit A letter authorizing a person or company to draw on a bank or stating that the bank will honor their credit up to the stated amount.

liability An accounting term signifying money owed or expected to be owed to another party. In law, a legal term signifying a legal obligation.

liability insurance Insurance covering the risks related to the property and personal liability claims of other parties against the insured party.

liberalization clause A clause in policies stating that if policies or endorsements currently in force are broadened by the passage of legislation or rulings from rating bodies, such policies or endorsements will be construed to include the broadening features.

license Generally, permission by a lawful authority to do an act that, without such permission, would be illegal. In real property, a privilege to enter for a specified purpose (for example, to collect rents), but does not confer on, or vest in, the licensee any title or estate in the property.

lien A legal hold or claim of a creditor on the property of another as security for a debt. Liens may be against real or personal property.

lien waiver A waiver of mechanic's lien rights; a document signed by a supplier or subcontractor stating that the firm has been compensated for its work, thereby giving up its right to file a claim against the property.

liquidation value The value of an asset upon its sale or disposition.

listing A written authorization for an agent to sell or lease real estate.

loan-to-value ratio (LTV) The ratio of amount borrowed to appraised value or sales price of real property expressed as a percentage.

loan transfer The assumption of existing financing by a new owner when a property is sold.

lockbox A postal address, maintained by the firm's bank, that is used solely for the purpose of collecting checks. A major goal of a lockbox is to reduce collection float, because the receipts are immediately credited to the firm's bank account.

loss draft Insurance payments in settlement of a claim for damage to mortgaged property. Drafts are generally made out to both the mortgagee and mortgagor.

loss of rents coverage *See* rental income insurance.

loss payable clause An insurance policy provision for the payment of a claim to someone other than the insured, who holds an insurable interest in the insured property.

loss payee The party named in a loss payable clause to whom insurance proceeds are to be paid in the event of damage to property in which the loss payee has an insurable interest. Loss payees include automobile lienholders and property mortgagees.

major tenants In commercial property, firms which are key lessees/tenants because of their high credit standing, the amount of space they occupy, and/or the percentage of gross rent they pay.

market Current supply and demand characteristics of a commodity in a given geographic/economic setting.

market approach to value In an appraisal, a market value estimate of the property based on actual prices paid in similar market transactions.

market rent The price a tenant pays a landlord for the use and occupancy of real property based on current rent for comparable property.

marketable title A title that may not be completely clear but has only minor objections that a well-informed and prudent buyer of real estate would accept.

market value The highest price that a buyer and the lowest price that a seller would accept, neither one being compelled to buy or sell. *See* fair market value.

master lease A lease under which the leasehold is further subleased by the tenant to one or more subtenants.

maturity The date on which an agreement expires; termination of a promissory note.

mechanic's lien A claim created by law to secure priority of payment for work performed and materials provided by a vendor. Land may be liened, as well as buildings, equipment, or other property.

menu pricing The method of service fee calculation where each function the servicer performs for the lender has a corresponding fee.

menu pricing fee Generally expressed in basis points ("bp") and calculated using the loan balance.

MIP (mortgage insurance premium) The amount paid by a mortgagor for mortgage insurance either to FHA or a private mortgage insurance company.

monetary default A breach or nonperformance of the terms of the note due to the nonpayment of debt service or escrow payments.

moratorium Legal authorization to delay the enforcement of liability for debt, or to suspend an activity.

mortgage A pledge of property, usually real property, as security for a debt; by extension, the document evidencing the pledge. In many states this document is a deed of trust. The document may contain the terms of repayment of the debt. By further extension, *mortgage* may be used to describe both the mortgage proper and the separate promissory note evidencing the debt and providing the terms of the debt's repayment.

mortgagee clause A clause that may be attached to an insurance policy stipulating that the lender will receive a portion of insurance proceeds sufficient to satisfy the unpaid amount of a loan in the event of a loss.

mortgagee The lender in a mortgage transaction.

mortgagee in possession A mortgagee who, due to default under the terms of a mortgage, has obtained possession but not ownership of the property.

MSA (metropolitan statistical area) A geographic area designated by the U.S. Census Bureau for purposes of collecting and disseminating demographic information.

NAIC (National Association of Insurance Commissioners) An organization whose membership consists of state insurance regulators and whose objectives are to promote uniformity in regulation by drafting model laws and regulations for adoption by the states and to provide support services to insurance departments such as examinations and statistical information.

named insured An individual, business, or organization specified in the declarations by name as the insured(s) under a policy.

named perils A policy that specifically lists the perils insured against, as opposed to an all risk policy that covers all perils other than those specifically excluded.

negative cash flow The deficit created when expenditures required to maintain an investment exceed income received on the property.

negotiable instrument Written order to pay, such as a check or promissory note, that may be transferred from one person to another provided certain conditions are met.

net effective rent The rental income generated by a lease computed over the life of the lease after deduction of total rent concessions and expressed as an annual dollar amount or annual dollar amount per square foot.

net rate The rate of interest remitted to an investor after servicing fees have been deducted from the gross rate.

net operating income (NOI) The amount remaining after total operating expenses (excluding interest payments) are deducted from effective gross income.

net realizable value An amount or figure resulting from the sale or disposition of property or an asset after all expenses associated with such sale or disposition are paid.

net rentable area The actual square footage of a building that can be rented (common areas, such as hallways, lobbies, elevator shafts, etc., are generally not included).

net worth The value of all assets, including cash, less total liabilities. Often used as an underwriting guideline to indicate creditworthiness and financial strength.

non-disturbance agreement An agreement that permits a tenant under a lease to remain in possession despite any foreclosure.

non-monetary default A breach or nonperformance of any of the terms or covenants of the loan documents other than debt service and escrow payments.

non-performing loan A loan that has not fulfilled one or more of the terms, covenants, conditions, or obligations required under the mortgage.

nonrecourse loan Type of loan that prohibits the lender from attempting to recover against the borrower (personally) if the security value for the loan falls below the amount required to repay the loan.

non-waiver provision A provision reserving to a lender every right under a document or at law not previously waived. *Note:* A general term for any kind of paper or document signed by a borrower that is an acknowledgment of the debt and is, by inference, a promise to pay. When the note is secured by a mortgage, it is called a mortgage note and the mortgagee is named as the payee.

occurrence An accident, including continuous or repeated exposure, that results in bodily injury or property damage neither expected or intended by the insured. Occurrence policies cover claims that occur during the policy period regardless of when the claim is made against the policy. *See* claims made.

occupancy rate The percentage of space or units that are leased or occupied.

open listing A written contract that does not allow one licensed real estate agent the exclusive right to sell a property for a specified time, but reserving the owner's right to sell the property alone without the payment of a commission.

open period The interval of time under a mortgage during which the loan can be prepaid.

operating statement *See* Income and Expense Statement.

operations and maintenance plan A plan adopted for maintaining and remediating a known or potential environmental condition, usually utilized in the context of asbestos contamination.

opinion letter A letter issued by an attorney containing legal opinions addressing a variety of legal issues.

partial payment Payment of only a portion of the required amount due including payments received without the late charge.

partial release An instrument discharging only a portion of the secured property from a lien.

partnership agreement A contract between a business association of two or more owners who share in the profits and losses of the business.

payment and performance bonds A bond to guarantee payment/performance of certain specified acts, such as the completion of construction of a property or the payment/cost thereof.

payoff letter A statement detailing the unpaid principal balance, accrued interest, outstanding late charges, legal fees, and all other amounts necessary to pay off the lender in full.

percentage rent Rent that is computed as a percentage of retail sales above a breakpoint and paid by tenants under typical retail leases.

Usually paid instead of or in addition to a specified minimum base rent.

perfection Perfection is frequently used in the context of a security interest and means those steps legally required to give a secured party an interest in property against a debtor's creditors.

performing loan A loan that has and continues to fulfill all of the terms, covenants, conditions, or obligations required under the mortgage.

personal injury Injury other than those arising out of bodily injury, such as false arrest, malicious prosecution, wrongful entry, eviction, libel, slander, or violation of privacy. The extent of such coverage may vary from policy to policy.

personal property Any property that is not real property. Also, "chattel."

Phase I environmental audit A basic study conducted to evaluate the environmental condition of real property and/or improvements.

Phase II environmental audit A study of the environmental condition of property/improvements that is more detailed and in-depth than a Phase I audit. May include groundwater testing or testing of soil.

plans and specifications Architectural and engineering drawings and specifications for construction of a building or project. They include a description of materials to be used and the manner in which they are to be applied.

pledge agreement An instrument pursuant to which a borrower will assign/pledge as collateral for a loan a security interest in certain types of property (e.g., stock, accounts, etc.).

plot plan A layout of improvements on a site, including their location, dimensions, and landscapes. It is generally a part of the architectural plan.

policyholder surplus The amount by which an insurance company's assets exceed its liabilities, as reported in its annual statement. For a stock insurer the policyholder surplus would be the sum of its capital and surplus; for a mutual insurer, the policyholder surplus equals the company's surplus.

portfolio The collection of loans held for servicing or investment.

power of sale A provision in a deed of trust or mortgage that empowers a trustee, without court order, to sell property in the event of default by the mortgagor and to apply the proceeds of the sale to satisfy the obligation, the costs of invoking the procedure, and the expenses of the sale.

premium The amount paid, often in addition to the interest, to secure a loan.

prepayment The payment of all or part of a mortgage debt before it is due.

prepayment penalty/prepayment premium A charge the mortgagor pays the mortgagee for the privilege to prepay the loan.

prepayment privilege The right given a borrower in the mortgage to pay all or part of a mortgage debt without penalty prior to its maturity.

present value The current value of cash received at a definite point or points in the future.

principal The original balance of money lent, excluding interest. Also, the remaining balance of a loan, excluding interest.

priority The order of precedence of liens against property or assets. Priority is usually established by filing or recordation of liens, but may be established by statute or agreement.

promissory note A written promise to pay a specific amount at a specified time.

proof of loss A formal statement by an insured to his insurer outlining the circumstances of a loss and the amount of damage being sought in compensation.

property inspection The physical review/evaluation of a property to determine its current structural condition, to report any deferred maintenance and/or environmental problems, and to verify leasing status.

property manager An individual or company responsible for the daily and long range management of the operations of a property.

purchase agreement A written agreement between a buyer and seller of real property, setting forth the price and terms of the sale.

real estate *See* real property.

real property Land and improvements permanently attached to it, such as buildings. In some states, this term is synonymous with the term *real estate.*

receiver An impartial person appointed by the court to administer properties involved in foreclosure or other litigation, to receive its rents and profits, and to apply or dispose of them at the direction of the court.

recourse loan A type of mortgage loan in which the lender's remedies in the event of borrower default are unlimited, extending beyond the property to the borrower's personal assets. In secondary marketing, loan that the lender must repurchase in the case of loan default or other defect.

redemption period The time allowed by law in some states during which mortgagors may buy back their foreclosed properties by paying the balance owed on their delinquent mortgages, plus interest and fees.

red flag A warning term used to indicate further analysis as warranted.

refinancing The repayment of a debt from the proceeds of a new loan, using the same property as security.

regulatory agency An arm of the state or federal government that has the responsibility to license, pass laws, regulate, audit, and monitor industry related issues (i.e., NAIC, FHLBB, HUD).

reinsurance The practice of one insurance company (the reinsurer) accepting risks or business from another insurer (the ceding company). It allows insurers to maintain a larger spread of risk and avoid large catastrophes.

release The discharging of secured property from a lien.

remediation The process by which contaminants are removed from a building or site.

remedy The means by which a right is enforced or the violation of a right is prevented, redressed, or compensated.

remittance report A report detailing the respective funds sent to the lender.

rent roll A list of tenants leasing a property that details terms of lease, area leased, and the amount of rent being paid.

rentable area The area of a property, measured in square feet, upon which rent can be collected.

rental concession A landlord's agreement to forgo part of the advertised rent in an effort to attract tenants.

rental income insurance A form of property insurance that pays the owner of a building (or other designated loss payee) for the amount of rent lost due to damage from an insured peril. Also, "loss of rents coverage."

replacement cost The cost to replace a structure with one of equivalent value and function but not necessarily identical in design or materials.

replacement cost endorsement An insurance endorsement used with a policy to insure that coverage is on a replacement cost basis.

replacement reserve A cash reserve for the replacement of fixed assets.

reserves Funded or non-funded accounts set up at either the property or portfolio level in anticipation of periodic or non-periodic capital expenditures or cash needs.

restructure A loan for which the basic terms, such as interest rate, maturity date, collateral, or guaranty have been modified as a result of actual or anticipated delinquency. *See* workout.

retainage (retention) The amount of payments withheld from contractors or subcontractors per contractual agreement to insure final and satisfactory completion of job.

satisfaction The discharge of an obligation by paying a party what it is due.

satisfaction of mortgage The recorded instrument the lender provides to evidence payment in full of the mortgage debt.

scope of work A description of the nature of service, activities, studies, jobs, or work to be undertaken by a party.

secondary financing A funding method using a loan secured by a second mortgage on a property. Sometimes used to refer to any financing technique other than equity and first mortgage debt.

secondary mortgage market The market where lenders and investors buy and sell existing mortgages or mortgage-backed securities, thereby providing greater availability of funds for additional mortgage lending.

security deposit A deposit of money by a tenant to a landlord to secure performance of a written or oral rental agreement (lease).

security document/security instrument Mortgage, or deed of trust, evidencing the pledge of real estate as collateral for the loan.

security interest The interest of a creditor in the security collateralizing an investment.

sequester of rents A court-related action by which rental income derived from property is ordered by the court to be deposited with and held by the clerk of the court or other governmental/court official.

servicing fee/servicing rate The fee earned by a servicer for administering a loan for an investor usually expressed as a percentage of the unpaid principal balance of the loan and deducted from the monthly mortgage payment.

servicing spread That portion of the interest rate added by the lender to cover the cost of administering the mortgage asset.

setback lines Lines that define the required distances for the location of a structure in relation to the perimeter of the property. They are in accordance with building codes, deed restrictions, and zoning requirements.

settlement statement *See* closing statement.

site plan A drawing that shows all improvements to a site, such as clearing, grading, and the installation of public utilities, before the actual construction of a building.

stabilization Measurement over a period of time to establish an average or expected outcome.

subcontractor A person or company contracted to perform work for a developer or general contractor.

subdivision Improved or unimproved land divided into a number of parcels for sale, lease, financing, or development.

sublease A lease executed by a lessee to a third person for a term no longer than the remaining portion of the original lease.

subordinate lien A lien or encumbrance (for example, a second mortgage or mechanic's lien) on real estate whose priority is inferior to another's recorded interest in the same property.

subordination agreement A document by which parties acknowledge, by written record, that the debt of one is inferior to the debt or interest of another in the same property. Subordination may apply not only to mortgages, but also to leases, real estate rights, and any other types of debt interests.

subordination (lease) provision A clause in a lease by which the tenant acknowledges that his or her interest in the lease premises is inferior to the interest of the lender whose mortgage encumbers the leased premises.

subrogation The right of a party to proceed against another for recovery.

super priority lien A lien or encumbrance on property that is superior to most every other claim against the same property irrespective of the time of recording or claiming the lien or encumbrance (usually arising in the context of liens for remediating hazardous waste).

superior lien A lien or encumbrance (for example, a mortgage or mechanic's lien) on real estate whose priority is greater (or superior) to the interest of another's interest in the same property.

survey A measurement of land, prepared by a registered land surveyor, showing the location of the land with reference to known points, its dimensions, and the location and dimensions of any improvements.

surveyor's certificate A formal statement, signed, certified, and dated by a surveyor, giving the pertinent facts about a particular property and any easements or encroachments affecting it.

tenant One who is not the owner but occupies real property under consent of the owner and in subordination to the owner's title. The tenant is entitled to exclusive possession, use, and enjoyment of the property, usually for a time and amount specified in the lease.

tenant improvements Constructed improvements to the base building, such as interior partitions, drop ceilings, and other finishes that prepare a space for occupancy and use by a tenant.

term The period of time between the commencement date and termination date of a note, mortgage, legal document, or other contract mortgage; it is called a mortgage note and the mortgagee is named as the payee.

third party One not a party to an agreement or a transaction, but who may have rights therein.

title binder Written evidence of temporary title insurance coverage that runs for a limited time and must be replaced by a permanent policy.

title exception An exclusion appearing in a title insurance policy against which the insurance company does not insure.

title insurance commitment *See* title binder.

title insurance policy A contract by which the insurer agrees to pay the insured a specific amount for any loss caused by defects of title to real estate, wherein the insured has an interest as purchaser, mortgagee, or otherwise.

title search An examination of public records, laws, and court decisions to ensure that no one except the seller has a valid claim to the property and to disclose past and current facts regarding ownership of the subject property.

title update An examination of public records from the date of a previous title search to ascertain the status of title to property since such last search.

transfer *See* assumption.

transfer fees Fees charged by an investor or servicer to process a transfer of ownership request.

umbrella insurance A type of policy obtained by an insured to cover loss or damage for a number of properties or other assets, or a number of companies (such as subsidiaries of a parent company).

underwriting criteria In mortgage banking, the analysis of the risk involved in making a mortgage loan to determine whether the risk is acceptable to the lender. Underwriting involves the evaluation of the property as outlined in the appraisal report, and of the borrower's ability and willingness to repay the loan.

uniform commercial code (UCC) A comprehensive code of laws regulating important legal aspects of business and financial transactions. The Code has been accepted by every state except Louisiana.

usable area The actual number of square feet contained within a tenant's demised space.

usury The act of charging borrowers a rate of interest greater than that permitted by law.

usury saving clause A clause in a loan document intended to protect the lender from a claim that an unlawful amount of interest is being charged.

utilities Basic services associated with developed areas that include provisions for electricity, telephone, gas, water, and garbage collection.

voluntary petition of bankruptcy A voluntary action filed under the United States Bankruptcy Code (the "Code") by a debtor seeking protection under the Code.

waiver of subrogation An endorsement issued by an insurer that waives its right of subrogation against a third party. It is usually requested by an insured in conjunction with a lease.

waiver of trial by jury provision A provision in a loan document whereby the borrower and/or lender waive their respective rights to a trial by jury in a legal action/lawsuit on a loan document.

waste An abuse or destructive use of property by one in rightful possession (such as an owner or tenant).

watchlist A list of loans that, while current in terms of monthly payments, pose a potential risk of loss due to deferred maintenance, delinquent real estate taxes, low debt service coverage, major lease expirations, or other signs of increasing financial stress on property performance.

working files The files used to store correspondence, insurance and tax information, mortgage document copies, and any other information used in the day-to-day servicing of a mortgage loan. Also commonly referred to as "servicing files."

workout An alternative action to foreclosure for the benefit of the lender and the borrower. Includes loan modification, short sales, and various forms of forbearance. *See* restructure.

yield maintenance The prepayment premium that will equal the present value of any costs to the lender resulting from the difference in interest rates between the date of the note and the date on which the prepayment is made.

zoning The creation of districts by local governments in which specific types of property uses are authorized.